TED HUGHES

A BEGINNER'S GUIDE

CHARLIE BELL

Series Editors
Rob Abbott & Charlie Bell

Hodder & Stoughton

A MEMBER OF THE HODDER HEADLINE GROUP

Dedication

To Di for her continual support, and to Barbara and Dennis Bell, my parents, whose long-term vision and encouragement led to this book.

Orders: please contact Bookpoint Ltd, 130 Milton Park, Abingdon, Oxon OX14 4SB. Telephone: (44) 01235 827720, Fax: (44) 01235 400454. Lines are open from 9.00–6.00, Monday to Saturday, with a 24-hour message answering service. Email address: orders@bookpoint.co.uk

British Library Cataloguing in Publication Data
A catalogue record for this title is available from The British Library

ISBN 0 340 84647 X

First published 2002
Impression number   10 9 8 7 6 5 4 3 2 1
Year   2007 2006 2005 2004 2003 2002

Cover photo from Jane Bown/Camera Press Ltd.
Typeset by Transet Limited, Coventry, England.
Printed in Great Britain for Hodder & Stoughton Educational, a division of Hodder Headline Plc, 338 Euston Road, London NW1 3BH by Cox & Wyman, Reading, Berks.

CONTENTS

How to use this book

The *Beginner's Guide* series aims to introduce readers to major writers of the past 500 years. It is assumed that readers will begin with little or no knowledge and will want to go on to explore the subject in other ways.

BEGIN READING THE AUTHOR

This book is a companion guide to Ted Hughes's major poetic works; it is not a substitute for reading the works themselves. Most of the poems mentioned will be found in *New Selected Poems*, (Faber & Faber, 1995). It would be useful if you read some of the poems in parallel, so that you can put theory into practice. This book is divided into sections. After considering how to approach the author's work and a brief biography, we go on to explore some of his main writings and themes before examining some critical approaches to the author. The survey finishes with suggestions for further reading and possible areas of further study.

HOW TO APPROACH UNFAMILIAR OR DIFFICULT TEXTS

Coming across a new writer may seem daunting, but do not be put off. The trick is to persevere. Much good writing is multi-layered and complex. It is precisely this diversity and complexity which makes literature rewarding and exhilarating.

Literary work often needs to be read more than once, and in different ways. These ways can include: a leisurely and superficial reading to get the main ideas and narrative; a slower more detailed reading focusing on the nuances of the text, concentrating on what appear to be key passages; and reading in a random way, moving back and forth through the text to examine such things as themes, narrative or characterization.

In complex texts it may be necessary to read in short chunks. When it comes to tackling difficult words or concepts it is often enough to guess in context on the first reading, making a more detailed study using a dictionary or book of critical concepts on later reading. If you prefer to look up unusual words as you go along, be careful that you do not disrupt the flow of the text and your concentration.

VOCABULARY
You will see that key terms and unfamiliar words are set in **bold** text. These words are defined and explained in the Glossary to be found at the back of the book.

ABBREVIATIONS USED IN THIS BOOK
The page numbers for Hughes's poems refer to:

BL	*Birthday Letters*	Faber & Faber 1998
GD	*Gaudete*	Faber & Faber 1977
HIR	*The Hawk in the Rain*	Faber & Faber 1957
MD	*Moortown Diary*	Faber & Faber 1989
NSP	*New Selected Poems*	Faber & Faber 1995
RCD	*Rain-Charm for the Duchy*	Faber & Faber 1992
TB	*Three Books*	Faber & Faber 1993

REFERENCES
Where bibliographical references are not given in full, these will be found in the Bibliography and Further Reading list at the end of the book.

Rob Abbott and Charlie Bell – Series Editors

Why Read Ted Hughes Today?

HE IS VERY POPULAR

Ted Hughes (1930–1998) is a phenomenon. His popularity is such that he is studied very widely from primary school to university research level. His prodigious output includes poetry, translations, literary criticism, radio broadcasts, children's books and plays.

HE HAS A UNIQUE VISION

For a generation brought up to believe that 'nature' poetry was gentle, harmonious and best typified by Wordsworth's 'The Daffodils', Hughes's poetry sticks rather refreshingly in the gullet. For in Hughes, nature is not gentle – it is raw, violent, unforgiving and compelling: horses steam and glisten; hawks watch coldly from the treetops rehearsing 'perfect kills'; winds stampede across fields; and crows become cruel cartoon characters who mock the Creator himself. Hughes has single-handedly redefined what we mean by a nature poet and what we understand by nature.

For Hughes, poetry and nature cannot be separated. In a world that is slowly being destroyed by humankind, his poetry mirrors the process and reflects the agony of ecological destruction.

To read Hughes is to be affected. No one who has read 'The Jaguar' can visit a zoo and look at the caged beasts and not recall Hughes's image of the jaguar 'hurrying enraged/ Through the prison darkness after the drills of his eyes', or Crow being born, 'trembling featherless elbows in the nest's filth'. In this sense Hughes's work can be disturbing. In the opening of *Gaudete*, over the course of just a few pages a man finds himself walking through a street lined with corpses and lying beneath a cow whilst it is butchered. This is not to imply that Hughes's poetry is sensationalist. Its effect is longer-lasting and more profound than that.

MYTHOLOGY AND LEGEND

Hughes's world is a place where life becomes legend and legend becomes life. He re-uses classical mythology to make more potent his own experiences. His imagery taps into our knowledge of fairy tale and myth, reconnecting us with a collective consciousness where the telling of tales and the creation of myths becomes part of our identity, and reaches deep into our often frightening subconscious. Hughes was a myth-maker, and as we shall see, his myths are powerful and profound.

Crow marked a turning point in Hughes's creative career, allowing him to express a more fully formed myth. In this collection his main character, Crow, lives in a dark yet comic world where God seems to have lost his way and where the mischievous, questing Crow stands for Everyman. As we shall see, *Crow* and later works use old and new mythology to explore the uneasy Cold War world of the mid-late twentieth century, as expressed through the pain and suffering of human beings and of Hughes himself.

HE HAS CHANGED THE WAY WE LOOK AT LANGUAGE

In the heady days when Hughes met and fell in love with Sylvia Plath, it seemed to them both that they could reshape the way language was used. Remarkably they seem to have been correct. The naked self-revelatory style of Plath's poetry was matched by the explosive violence of Hughes's work. The Ted Hughes style developed into what at first seems something very dry. Further study reveals that the language carries much meaning and bears much philosophical weight. His use of language is breathtaking and exciting.

The best effects are often formed by the clash of juxtaposition. A sample from *Crow* will demonstrate the shocking and often violent use of language:

> Cars collide and erupt luggage and babies
> In laughter
> The steamer upends and goes under saluting like a stuntman
> In laughter

('In Laughter', *Crow*, NSP p. 102)

Here, images are linked in frightening and disturbing ways. The way babies are spewed out like the luggage demonstrates the apparent indifference of Nature or God to the plight of human beings. The poem develops the idea by concentrating on the laughter itself, allowing it to get more and more out of control until it at last exhausts itself, and waits, with long pauses, 'Like somebody the police have come for'. Life is a tragi-comedy and Hughes is one of its most astute chroniclers.

HE HELPS SHED LIGHT ON THE WORK OF SYLVIA PLATH

After Sylvia Plath's suicide in 1963, Ted Hughes was left to pick up the pieces. He inherited her estate and became her editor and anthologist. Being an intensely private man he tried to keep people away from the painful story which had been their life together. He did this at the cost of much public disapprobation from people who blamed him for his wife's death. He suffered much pain at this time as he could not reply to his critics without injuring Plath's memory and blighting the lives of his two children.

However, near to death himself, Hughes surprised the world in 1998 by releasing *Birthday Letters*, a series of poems which chronicled his relationship with Plath. At last the world could begin to appreciate other sides to the picture, for the poems were a poignant and moving tribute to their life together. The release of other personal papers has also helped to give a broader picture of this crucial literary and emotional union.

✳ ✳ ✳ *SUMMARY* ✳ ✳ ✳

Ted Hughes is a giant of the twentieth century:

- He remains very popular

- He reinvents the use of myth and legend to make it relevant today

- He is essentially an eco-critic, mirroring the follies of human destruction

- He has redefined how language can be used

- He can shed light on Sylvia Plath.

2 Biography and Influences

EARLY YEARS

Ted Hughes was born on 17 August 1931 in Mytholmroyd, Yorkshire, to Edith and William Hughes. The town is in the Calder Valley near Hebden Bridge and the countryside is rugged and stark, set in the moorland landscape of the Pennines. Hughes lived there with his family (sister Olwyn, two years his senior and brother Gerald, ten years older than Ted). This appears to be have been a happy and formative time for Hughes and he would stalk the moors, often with Gerald, observing everything and soaking it all up. The starkness of the landscape and the phlegmatic Yorkshire temperament came to pervade his character.

In 1938 the family moved to the mining town of Mexborough. Ted was not put out by this move and, although his brother left home, Ted continued to go out on his own, stalking animals and observing their behaviour.

At both places he was brought up against startling or surprising happenings, such as meeting extremely close with a fox, or a tramp, and soaking up bizarre local stories.

In 1943 Ted went to Mexborough Grammar School where he began to write comic verse for his classmates and where some of his teachers began to foster his poetic gift. He had several poems published in the school magazine before winning an Open Exhibition to Pembroke College, Cambridge.

CAMBRIDGE AND AFTER

Before taking up his scholarship, Hughes did his two years' National Service in the RAF as a radio mechanic. He spent most of his time at an isolated station with two other men and, to alleviate the boredom, read and re-read Shakespeare, eventually being able to quote great chunks of it by heart.

He had hoped that studying literature at Cambridge would help him as a poet, but instead he found his creative impulses being stifled and did not make a good scholar. His disenchantment with English studies led him to change to reading archaeology and anthropology and he graduated in 1954. During his time at Cambridge he did manage to read some folk tales and a lot of Yeats and even wrote a few poems, some of which got published in a magazine called *Chequer* and one of which, 'The Little Boy and the Seasons', was published in *Granta*.

Following university, Hughes went through several casual jobs including rose gardener, night watchman, teacher, reader for Arthur J. Rank and, most notably, at a local zoo. It is obvious from Hughes's work that the zoo provided him with a chance of close-up observation of some of the animals, including a restless jaguar which later turned up in 'Jaguar' in *Hawk in the Rain*, but according to biographer Elaine Feinstein, he spent more time washing up in the cafeteria than being with the animals.

SYLVIA PLATH

Some of Hughes's friends decided to launch a new magazine called *St Botolph's Review* and published several of his poems in the first issue. At the launch party on 26 February 1956, Hughes met a pretty young American called Sylvia Plath. She was at Cambridge as a Fulbright scholar and was already an accomplished poet after winning several poetry competitions. Hughes recounts their first meeting in dramatically ironic style:

> First sight. First snapshot isolated
> Unalterable, stilled in the camera's glare.
> Taller
> Than you ever were again. Swaying so slender
> It seemed your long, perfect, American legs
> Simply went on up …
> And the face – a tight ball of joy.

> ('St Botolph's', BL p. 14)

They fell for each other very quickly and were married on 16 June 1956. The only guest was Plath's mother, who accompanied them on their honeymoon in Benidorm, at a time when it was a sleepy Spanish village. When Hughes looked back in *Birthday Letters*, he could already see that there were chasms of difference between them, but for the first few years of their married life, they generally got on well and supported each other's efforts to write and get published.

Hughes and Plath on honeymoon in Paris.

FIRST SUCCESS

Later in 1956 Plath typed up Hughes's *The Hawk in the Rain* manuscript and entered it for an unlikely sounding competition. The sponsor was the Poetry Centre of the Young Man's and Young Women's Hebrew Association of New York, and the prize was to be publication by Harper. Hughes won and the collection was published, to much critical acclaim, in September 1957.

The couple moved to America, and Plath took up teaching at Smith College, Northampton, Massachusetts, while Hughes wrote and taught a term of Creative Writing and English at the University of Massachusetts. Later, in 1958, the couple met artist Leonard Baskin and his wife. From this came a strong collaborative partnership between Hughes and Baskin which led to the latter illustrating *Crow*, *Cave Birds* and many other books. Soon after this Plath decided to give up paid employment so that she could concentrate on writing.

UPS AND DOWNS

The couple returned to London, via a short stay in Heptonstall, and eventually came to live in a cramped flat in Primrose Hill, London. They remained relatively poor throughout their marriage. Hughes kept himself busy writing reviews, articles, essays and a series of talks for the BBC's *Listening and Writing* programme, as well as continuing to write his poems. London at that time was a heady place for young artists and writers and there was a thriving literary scene, partially centred on, and fostered by, the BBC. In April 1960 their first child Frieda was born, followed by Nicholas in January 1962. Hughes was busy on all sorts of projects and especially on the *Crow* collection for which he was doing much research as well as writing, and had boxes full of papers. The marriage does not seem to have been an easy affair, particularly as Plath seemed to be excessively jealous for her husband's attention, and in particular hated it if he ever met another woman for whatever reason (though she never appeared jealous of his writing successes). Both partners appear to have been intensely moody.

In August 1961, the Hughes family moved to a house they had bought in Devon called Court Green. It was by all accounts an idyllic place and it became a major project as it needed much care and attention. It was a time of success for both Sylvia and Ted, and marked a fruitful period in their literary lives.

ASSIA WEVILL

In May 1962, Hughes and Plath had a visit from David and Assia Wevill, to whom they had sublet the Primrose Hill flat. Hughes became infatuated by Assia and an affair developed which broke the Hughes's marriage and ended in separation. Plath asked Hughes to leave Court Green, which he did. A frenzied bout of writing by Plath followed in a series of poems which were published posthumously in *Ariel*. The couple's efforts at reconciliation were unsuccessful. There was a final separation when Hughes stayed with friends in London.

TRAGEDY

Plath bought a flat in London and attempted to set up a new life there. Depression set in. On 11 February 1963 she tucked up the two children in bed, phoned a babysitter, left a note for her doctor and then gassed herself. It is unclear if she meant to commit suicide or whether it was a cry for help. Hughes was devastated and ceased writing poems for some time. The *Crow* project was left unfinished and the available poems were collected and published as *Crow* in 1970.

For several years after the tragedy, Hughes wrote little for adults but chose instead to write for children. Both *How the Whale Became* and *The Earth-Owl and Other Moon-People* were published in November 1963 and were to be the precursors of much other writing for children, including the much loved *The Iron Man* in 1968. Hughes became executor of Plath's estate and he set about publishing her poems and protecting her memory and his children's privacy. *Ariel* was published, to some consternation, in 1965, and many criticized the order that he had chosen for the poems, and his omission of some poems which were harsh about himself. Thus began a long period during which Hughes was silent on the subject of her death, and a rising tide of vilification whereby he was blamed for her death and Plath became a feminist icon and martyr.

COLLABORATION WITH PETER BROOK

At around this time Hughes began a fruitful series of collaborations with Peter Brook and the National Theatre Company, beginning with a reworking of Seneca's *Oedipus*, first performed in March 1968, eventually leading to a trip to Iran to help Brook's *International Centre for Theatre Research* in the Shiraz Festival of 1971. Hughes's experiments led to his creation of a new language (Orghast) with which the actors tried to communicate beyond words. It was an attempt to gain freedom from the fetters and misinterpretations of ordinary language, and to set up cross-cultural theatre.

FURTHER TRAGEDY

In March 1969 an unhappy Assia gassed herself and her daughter Shura. This was followed by the death of Hughes's mother in May. These were terrible blows from which it took Hughes a long time to recover. He bought Lumb Bank near Hebden Bridge as a further property in which to work but moved around between several homes including Court Green.

SETTLING DOWN

In August 1970 Hughes married Carol Orchard, daughter of Jack, a neighbouring farmer in Devon. He decided to put down roots in Devon and began a new career as a farmer in collaboration with Carol and Jack. On 12 October, *Crow* was published.

Farming suited Hughes and he came to enjoy the feeling of being with the elements. It was a world of the heart, not the head, and its raw quality appealed to him. He began to write a series of journal pieces which eventually became *Moortown Diary*. Essentially he retreated from the world, enjoying farming and writing. There he could remain private and concentrate on his many projects. Jack died in 1974 and is commemorated in *Moortown Diary*. Hughes still spent a lot of time in London during the week, and according to Elaine Feinstein, his biographer, carried on at least one long-term affair (with Jill Barber). His marriage with Carol continued despite this.

POET LAUREATE

In 1984 Hughes received a special honour when he was appointed Poet Laureate after the death of the previous incumbent, Sir John Betjeman. He took this work seriously and produced enough poems to fill a collection called *Rain-Charm for the Duchy*.

FINAL YEARS

Hughes's subsequent output was prodigious and continued right up to his death in 1998. Late in his life he decided to publish a series of poems he had written over the years about his relationship with Sylvia Plath. His *Birthday Letters* appeared in January 1998 and began a new debate which allowed his side of the story to be aired. On the basis that the adverse comments of his detractors had caused him great pain, the release of the poems just before his death was timely and largely welcomed.

Ted Hughes died of cancer on Wednesday 28 October 1998.

SERVICES TO WRITING, AND ACCOLADES

Hughes was a relentless worker in the cause of literature and served on many literary panels, competitions, and conferences. His major contribution to the lives of fellow and aspiring writers was his support for the **Arvon Foundation**, to which he devoted himself.

KEY FACT

Arvon Foundation: Exists to give writing courses to aspiring writers led by published writers. Lumb Bank is now one of the Arvon centres.

The list of prizes and awards he received is long, and includes the Hawthornden Prize (1961), the City of Florence International Poetry Prize (1969), the Queen's Gold Medal for Poetry (1974), the Guardian Children's Fiction Award (1984 and 1985), the Whitbread Award (1997) and the Forward Prize (1998), plus many more.

INFLUENCES

In the January 1971 edition of *London Magazine*, Hughes gave an interview to Egbert Fass in which he discussed the main influences on his work. In it he mentions William Blake, John Donne, Dylan Thomas, D. H. Lawrence, Gerard Manley Hopkins, W. B. Yeats, T. S. Eliot, Chaucer and Shakespeare among others. All of these poets shared a passion for the landscape, nature and man's relationship to it. He also acknowledges his debt to the German philosopher Artur **Schopenhauer** and mentions other influences such as *The Tibetan Book of the Dead*, which fuelled much of his thinking and formed a part of his study of magic and the occult (see 'Hughes the shaman', p. 20). Hughes and Plath often used a ouija board through a spirit messenger they called Pan, partly to fuel Plath's muse and in an attempt to heal her feelings of loss for her father, and partly as a way for Hughes to continue his study of the darker side of existence.

KEY FACT

Schopenhauer (1788–1860): Emphasized the active role of the Will as the creative but hidden force in human nature and thus founded a movement whose influence reached far down history through Nietzsche and Freud. The 'Will' referred to is a complex idea but basically is an all-pervading force which rules the whole of life. It is unconscious and unknowable; we can only experience it. The Will contains an inner antagonism that leads to a never-ending war of extermination and a struggle between various powerful forces. The Will is basically a flux of competing forces, with no driving purpose or limits. It just *is*.

Robert Graves's book *The White Goddess* greatly influenced Hughes's thinking and helped to form a set of ideas on which he was to work throughout his life. We will look at its importance in Chapter 4.

Eastern European poets such as Vasko Popa, Miroslav Holub and Zbigniew Herbert also interested Hughes. Theirs was poetry with a political edge, born out of the Second World War and its barbarity, against a background of state totalitarianism. Hughes admired their improvised language and their disregard for convention in writing.

One major influence on Hughes's writing was Sylvia Plath herself. The couple took a great interest in each other's work and there was a fruitful crossover of ideas, especially about language. This is seen most clearly in *Birthday Letters* because many of the poems are based on Plath's poems, or allude to them.

✳ ✳ ✳ *SUMMARY* ✳ ✳ ✳

● Hughes began writing quite early in life.

● His marriage to Sylvia Plath led to some fine poetry from both parties but ended in tragedy when she committed suicide.

● His relationship with Assia Wevill also ended tragically in her suicide.

● Hughes remarried and became reclusive, trying to shield himself and his family from the legacy of his first marriage while combining writing with farming in Devon.

● He became Poet Laureate in 1984.

● He died of cancer in 1998, already a legend and regarded as the finest English poet of his generation.

How to Approach Ted Hughes 3

Ted Hughes's poetry can be accessed in the same way as much other modern poetry. That is to say, it requires some effort and careful study to reveal its depth and subtlety although much can still be gained from a first reading. The trick is to look beyond the language and symbols he uses.

CONTEXT

Hughes can be seen in the context of a long tradition of poets stretching back at least as far as the Romantics. Poetry in the twentieth century largely became a reaction against the **Romantic movement** (or at least, the Romantics' treatment of their subject), and the perceived tweeness of **Georgian** poetry. In an age of industrialized mass warfare, dominated by the ideas of Freud, Jung, Einstein and Marx, the way the human race perceived itself changed. The world became less certain and belief in a beneficent God waned.

Literature became more conscious of the fragmented nature of life and its desperate uncertainties. By the time Hughes began to write, the first upheaval of **modernism** was over, or was at least settling down and there seemed a need to think again about the way poetry was going. A new wave of poets called the **Movement** had risen to attention but their poetry was hardly what you would call wild. In 1964, in his introduction to *The New Poetry*

KEYWORDS

Georgian: A term now used pejoratively to refer to the worst of poetry written in the early twentieth century. Such poetry is much criticized for its pastoral and escapist style.

Modernism: In literature, a broad movement of writers including T. S. Eliot, Pound, Joyce, Woolf, Yeats and D. H. Lawrence. It was informed by the works of Freud and was characterized by a persistent experimentation with language and form. Stream of consciousness is one of its major techniques as well as dependence upon poetic image and myth.

Romantic movement: A movement in Britain and Europe roughly between 1770 and 1848. In literary terms it expressed the self

(Penguin, 1962), poet A. Alvarez issued a challenge to English poets to engage in what he called 'in depth' poetry, famously comparing 'At Grass' by Philip Larkin with a Hughes poem from *The Hawk in the Rain* called 'A Dream of Horses'. Alvarez's conclusion was that Hughes's poem was 'about something', rather than being a mere description of something – it avoided what Alvarez considered to be an intellectual gentility inherent in English poetry which prevented strong poetry from developing.

Hughes's poetry is certainly 'about something', and that is why he has become so popular. As we shall see, he was exploring how myth and legend could be used in new ways to express life as he saw it. He also makes much use of symbol and follows the tradition of William Blake, and W. B. Yeats in this respect.

and the value of individual experience along with a strong sense of the transcendental. The movement is characterized by such writers as Rousseau, Wordsworth, Mary Wollstonecraft, Coleridge, Byron and Shelley. The motif of the movement was 'Imagination' and it had a belief in the close links between man and nature. In this sense, Hughes is in the Romantic tradition but his imagery and vision are much more savage.

The Movement: A post-war movement of British poets whose poetry is sardonic, lucid and self-consciously ironic. '...meticulously crafted and witty, controlled and common-sensical' (*Bloomsbury Guide to English Literature*, 1989). The major poets include Thom Gunn, Elizabeth Jennings, Philip Larkin and John Wain.

TACKLING HUGHES'S POETRY

Take several readings

Hughes's poetry is dense and the ideas are compressed. Each poem requires to be read at least two or three times and usually more. On the first reading it is helpful to jot down some first impressions of your thoughts and feelings. Although you may get a sense of what the poem is 'about', it is wise not to form too certain a view at this point.

On subsequent readings you can study different aspects of the poem, such as the rhythmical and rhyming patterns, the images and symbols used, and the overall feeling, as well as formulating some ideas about what the poem is expressing.

Read aloud

After Hughes's death, Alistair Niven, Director of Literature at the British Council, wrote a tribute in which he commented on Hughes's outstanding gift as a reader of poetry.

> He was without question the finest verse reader I have ever heard…
> The voice was baritone, inflected by Yorkshire, always strong, clear and musical.
>
> ('Tributes to Ted Hughes', *Literature Matters 25* at
> www.britishcouncil.org/arts/literature/literature_matters_25/hughes.htm)

Hughes's work benefits from being read aloud. You can discover more closely the shape and rhythm of a poem, and can often unleash more of its power. If you can get hold of recordings of Hughes reading his work, this too will help.

Read more than one poem at a sitting

Hughes often themes his work, so by reading a batch together you can begin to discover a bigger picture. This is obvious in such collections as *Crow* but can be found in most of his collections. Even when you are reading poems in a selected collection of his work, it will still pay to read more than one poem at a time.

Try to avoid looking for meaning

In a collection like *Lupercal*, you may find one poem crystal clear while the next seems so dense that it seems impossible to extract a meaning. In this case, you must come to terms with the words as best you can. Often, the search for meaning is fruitless. It is better to read the poem in a less focused way, concentrating on striking words and images, letting these play on the subconscious mind. Usually, something strikes you about a poem which can help you to appreciate it more. It can also be helpful to read some academic literature about Hughes's work. Some of the more helpful texts are mentioned throughout this book.

A reading of 'The Thought-Fox'

In order to get a flavour for Hughes's work, you now need to read a copy of his poem 'The Thought-Fox' (NSP p. 3) several times as described previously on p. 15.

This is Hughes's first animal poem, a poem remarkable for its great popularity and its appearance in many anthologies. It appeared in Hughes's first collection *The Hawk in the Rain*, and Hughes ascribed enough importance to it to put it first in his *New Selected Poems*.

Tackling the subject

'The Thought-Fox' demonstrates much of what Hughes tries to do in a poem. It is, first and foremost, an animal poem. The fox depicted is one that Hughes recollected as a childhood memory after a year barren of creativity. The poem brings us very close to the fox by the use of fine detail, and we can see its nose touching twigs and leaves, the eyes criss-crossing the midnight grass until we catch one eye much closer, 'A widening deepening greenness'. The fox is a very powerful presence and we experience the closeness of the encounter by 'a sudden sharp hot stink of fox'. Those who have observed foxes will know and understand that sense of a fox 'coming about its own business'.

'The Thought Fox' at work.

Leaping poetry

In *Poetry in the Making*, Hughes described the poem as being 'about a fox, obviously enough, but a fox that is both a fox and not a fox'. The fox becomes a metaphor as the poem proceeds. Its furtive and purposeful actions suddenly transform themselves into the poem itself. We are surprised by the sudden twist, the transformation from fox to thought-fox, and the sudden revelation of a poem on a page. We become aware that the 'I' of 'I imagine' in the first line is the writer: not merely the passive observer of a piece of rural life. The observer is the writer without an idea, lonely in 'this midnight moment's forest'. But we were not aware of this when we first read the first lines of the poem. A transcendence has taken place, what Robert Bly calls a 'leap':

> The real joy of poetry is to experience this leaping inside the poem. A poem which is 'leaping' makes a jump from an object soaked in unconscious substance to an object or idea soaked in conscious psychic substance ...
>
> (Robert Bly, *Leaping Poetry*, Beacon Press, 1975)

Use of metaphor

Hughes uses his subjects in exactly this way. They become metaphors which leap to connect with other associations or with myth and legend. Once the fox has become a metaphor, then its footprints suddenly become the 'neat prints' of the printed word.

Form

Form is very important to Hughes. You will notice in this poem the tight four-line structure of the stanzas, the effortless **half-rhymes** – star/near; snow/hollow; alive/move (surprisingly); greenness/business; and so on. The structure is irregular enough to keep the

KEYWORD

Half-rhyme: Basically a rhyme which does not match perfectly but contains enough syllables or consonants to create a similar sound pattern. Largely a twentieth-century device to avoid the irritation sometimes caused by exactly 'chiming' rhymes.

Metaphor: A poetic device whereby an object or image comes to represent something it is not but with which it shares seemingly common characteristics. The slyness of a fox and its 'aliveness', its sense of purpose and individuality, can come to represent thoughts entering the brain of a poet.

reader wary but strong enough to carry the meaning along. As you read, take at least a passing interest in the structure, if only to get a sense of how he breaks his lines and decides on a form for his subject.

* * *SUMMARY* * *

Coming to terms with Hughes's poetry entails:

- Reading the poems several times and aloud if possible

- Reading them for things other than meaning

- Reading several poems at the same time to get the bigger picture

- Developing the ability to unpack dense language and learning to 'leap' with the writer

- Understanding how the poet uses metaphor, myth and legend to add force to the poems

- Taking an interest in the form of the poems.

Major Themes and Preoccupations

HUGHES THE SHAMAN

Hughes had a very clear idea of his role as a writer or bard. As part of his studies of other cultures and the **occult** he became fascinated by the idea of the **shaman**. As a shaman a poet can tap into areas that others can't or won't, and can challenge the reader by uncovering what has been buried in the collective unconscious. By the time we get to *Crow*, we can sense that Hughes is moving below the usual psychic surface of humanity, bringing to light elements from our collective and often suppressed unconscious. That is why the poetry can often seem difficult or uneasy – the shaman is working his magic.

KEYWORDS

Shaman: In tribal cultures, someone who has tested himself to the utmost limits, has shed everything about himself, and has come back as a visionary and healer, exploring the spiritual unconsciousness of the tribe he serves.

Cabbalah: A system of symbol and number based on the Jewish mystical scheme of theology and metaphysics.

Hughes's ideas were based on those of Claude Lévi-Strauss. The idea explored is that modern and ancient minds, at an unconscious level, vary very little. Each civilization sets up a series of representations which underlie it and which are carried forward unconsciously through the generations. This is why symbols and stories from the past can still affect the modern reader.

THE OCCULT

The fascination for the world of the occult led Hughes to read widely about it. He was interested in exploring the energies which lay behind life, and his investigation included a study of alchemy and the **Cabbalah**. In an interview with Egbert Fass (*London Magazine*, January 1971) Hughes tried to qualify the use of the word 'violent' about his work, by looking at his two jaguar poems from *The Hawk in the Rain*. Hughes describes a jaguar in several different ways and then, drawing on his belief in the supernatural, adds: 'Or he is simply a demon ... a lump of ectoplasm. A lump of astral energy ... the tradition is, that energy of this sort once invoked will destroy an impure nature and serve a pure one.' Many of Hughes's poems contain elements of this, particularly in the earlier works.

MAN GOING WRONG

In *The Iron Man*, Hughes's fable for children, a giant robot comes to terrorize a community. It eats rolls of barbed wire as if they were spaghetti and munches tractors as if they were chocolate bars. Technology appears to have gone mad. The iron man acts without compassion and without motive. He eats to survive. Luckily for the villagers, this is a children's story, so a young boy called Hogarth befriends the monster and turns his strengths towards fighting the terrible Space-bat-angel-dragon, and all ends well.

The Iron Man gives us a clue to one of Hughes's concerns: the way Western society is slowly losing its sense of where man fits into the scheme of things. Human egocentricity and arrogance represent a kind of **nihilism**. This leads to a loss of faith in organized religion and is replaced by an insatiable curiosity which

> **KEYWORD**
>
> Nihilism: A denial of traditional values, including moral and social ones, which threatens to topple a prevailing order.

leads man to destroy things in an effort to understand them, a trait particularly to be found in the character of Crow, whom we will meet shortly.

Much of Hughes's work can be seen to be set in a post-Fall Garden of Eden. The fruits of knowledge have turned out to be much more complex than anyone might have imagined, and the psychological reverberations serve to show that we have still not found a satisfactory way of resolving them.

THE SUBJUGATION OF THE FEMININE

Where has man gone wrong? Part of Hughes's answer is to be found in Robert Graves's *The White Goddess*, especially the notion that there was once a controlling matriarchal principle in nature but that it has been suppressed by classical Greek mythologists. Hughes often alludes to this spirit in nature even when the imagery and language seem masculine.

Terry Gifford and Neil Roberts give us a good account of this nature goddess:

> This myth holds, in a single, imaginative unit, the total, inescapable character of reality, both beneficent and destructive. It assists Hughes in extending the perception of Wordsworth to incorporate all that is terrifying and predatory, as well as comforting and nurturing, in nature ... The Goddess is not separate from the world of things, and she is present in the human unconscious, accessible to disciplined techniques of imagination, states of meditation, ecstasy, extremes of anguish or bliss.

> (Gifford and Roberts, *Ted Hughes A Critical Study*)

A SENSE OF FOREBODING

It is no coincidence that the Iron Man has to climb a cliff from the beach before he can begin his feeding foray. Hughes himself, in *Writers on Themselves* (Cox & Wyman, 1964), describes how his early childhood affected all of his work. In Mytholmroyd, the village where he lived for the first seven years of his life, he remembers there being a large, overbearing 'cliff' which seemed to loom over his life – 'the dark, hairy wall of Scout Rock'. It has a sense of heaviness and foreboding about it. As he grew older, he and his older brother climbed it, but instead of gaining a sense of freedom and release upon reaching the top, the young Ted remembers looking down and finding his village so small below him that he couldn't distinguish his house. Elsewhere he was to find himself confronted by a vast expense of Yorkshire moors, spreading out to the horizon. The moors surrounded the little valley and hemmed him in. The character of the moors also affected him, being paradoxically both gloomy and exultant. Much of his poetry could be said to be expressing this sense of gloom and exultation, tempered by the temperament of the people and the place. He describes Yorkshire people 'as if they were only half-born from the earth, and the graves are too near the surface' (op. cit. p. 92). This might indeed be an apt description of Hughes himself, as seen through his poetry.

His brother Gerald told him stark stories about what happened on the cliff: a tramp shot, mistaken for a fox; a wood pigeon shot, but soaring, dead, across the sky, until it crashed into the valley on the other side. These dark tales are the very stuff of Hughes's work. They describe an imperfect world where things happen without warning or explanation.

LOSS AND LACK

A lot of Hughes's work can be said to be a study of what has become known as 'lack'.

> **KEYWORD**
>
> Lack: A feeling of missing something we greatly value. In the child it is the absence of the mother figure, and in adults it is anything which we feel makes us less than whole.

Theorists such as Kristeva and Lacan postulate that as a young child is fully dependent on its mother for the first months of its life, bonded to her in such a way that it feels a lack of her when she is not present. Further, the child does not know if the mother is ever going to return.

This sense of 'lack', and the fear evoked, pervades our lives and imbues us with a sense of loneliness and loss. The question is, how can we be sure of anyone or anything? How do we know that the desired object will return?

In C. S. Lewis's *Shadowlands* one of the characters quotes his father as saying 'We read to know we are not alone.' We are all engaged in this quest. We need to ensure that our sense of lack can be ameliorated by knowing that others exist (even in the imagination) – that they share something of our lives and also experience similar things.

Unfortunately, as we know when we try to console a bereaved friend, we cannot fully express our sorrow because we cannot fathom just how deep the sense of loss really is. We sense the 'lack' which lies behind the deep grief of the bereaved, but we also sense the 'lack' which lies behind our words. Hughes was deeply aware of this gulf between experience and language.

THE INADEQUACY OF LANGUAGE

In order to describe something we reach for language and, in particular, for words. We rely on words to help us to capture what we are trying to describe. We say that words have 'meaning', and assume that if these discrete 'meanings' can be strung together in the right way, then we will all share a common understanding of the intended meanings.

The big problem here is that an object can be described in many different ways. Certain linguists refer to the object being described as the 'signified', and the word used to describe the object as the 'signifier'. In the case of a dog (the signified), we know that in French it is known as a *chien*, in Portuguese a *cão*, (confusingly, pronounced similarly to the English 'cow') and so on. So the signifier in some strange way cannot be connected to the signified. And what kind of a dog is it, and what characteristics of dogginess are meant by the word dog? A dog to a working shepherd is a very different beast from a lapdog, requiring very different ways of thinking about and treating the animal.

Hughes was absorbed by this dilemma:

> There are no words to capture the infinite depth of crowiness in a crow's flight. All we can do is use a word as an indicator, or a whole bunch of words as a general directive. But the ominous thing in the crow's flight, the bare-faced, bandit thing, the tattered beggarly gipsy thing, the caressing and shaping yet slightly clumsy gesture of the downstroke, as if the wings were too heavy and too powerful, and the headlong sort of merriment, the macabre pantomime ghoulishness and the undertaker sleekness – you could go for a very long time with phrases of that sort

and still have completely missed your instant, glimpse knowledge of the world of the crow's wingbeat. And a bookload of such descriptions is immediately rubbish when you look up and see a crow flying.

(Hughes, *Poetry in the Making*, Faber, 1967)

If language cannot stand close scrutiny, how best can a poet come to terms with the apparent need to express the deep truths that lie behind the barrier of words? For Hughes, there was a desire to get beyond that barrier and to reveal what is 'real'.

When working on *Crow*, Hughes tells us, he was seeking to find 'a super-simple, and a super-ugly language which would … shed everything'. This language is often fragmented and apparently unstructured, but tries to find the real through its gaps (in this example from 'Crow's Vanity', he actually introduces typographical gaps too):

> Looking close in the evil mirror Crow saw
> Mistings of civilisations   towers   gardens
> Battles he wiped the glass   but there came
> Mistings of skyscrapers   webs of cities

THE SEARCH FOR THE REAL

What is it, then, that lies beyond the barrier of language? What are the experiences that are so indescribable, and why should one try to capture them? Hughes lived in an age where the old Judaeo-Christian orthodoxy of Western culture was becoming less relevant and yet there was still a need to express the feeling of 'Otherness', the strong and all-pervading forces which control our lives: birth, death, war, cruelty, pain, joy, rapture, love and so on. For many, God had ceased to be a plausible explanation of these 'real' occurrences, as we shall see when we come to look at *Crow* later on.

For Hughes, the world of animals can represent the Real. They seem to possess primeval forces and desires. They are strong in themselves and embody the Real simply because they are a part of the bloody, tragic, 'dog eat dog' continuum which is nature itself. Animals such as bulls, crows, foxes and owls pepper Hughes's work because he finds that they embody aspects of the Real which he is trying to explore.

In 'Pike' (NSP p. 41), a much anthologized poem from *Lupercal*, the powerful sense of menace partly comes from the unknown. The fish seem to possess a power we cannot comprehend. In an everyday sense the pike frighten us because their motives remain unspoken and their power simply 'is'.

The pike are 'a hundred feet long in their world', and Hughes likens them to sinister submarines. He talks of one pike he fished for in terms of high gothic horror. The pond he fished in was 'deep as England' and 'held pike too immense to stir'. As he casts his line, the hair melodramatically freezes on his head. The act of fishing carries a sense of real danger. It is as if Hughes is plumbing deep into the Real, or, in other terms, into the deep recesses of the unconscious mind. The poem has a sense of the nightmarish about it. He sets it in the 'dream/ Darkness beneath night's darkness', and thus manages to get as close to a definition of the Real in the human psyche as anyone is likely to get. The whole poem stands as a metaphor for the way man perceives himself, looking deep into a fathomless pond, a pond so deep that it encompasses all forms of the Real in all their frightening manifestations.

Notice too the mercilessness of the pike he keeps in a fish tank, the one eating the other two – a meaningless act to us, the observers, who nonetheless try to find meaning behind it.

Hughes's version of the Real links to the work of Jacques Lacan, and in particular, Lacan's beliefs about the nature of the unconscious mind and its links with the collective unconscious, language, and desires brought about by the growing sense of self in the child. Thus the Real is both an outer world and an inner nature.

THE HEALING POWER OF THE IMAGINATION

Hughes was interested in the idea of **individuation**. Much of his work is concerned with how man can achieve a wholeness, a oneness, through a process consisting of a series of trials. In this he is in accord with Carl Jung, who considered the process of individuation to be one of the tasks of middle age. As Hughes grew older his poetry began to show signs that he thought that wholeness could be achieved, and that suffering could be for a purpose.

> **KEYWORD**
>
> Individuation: A Jungian concept which describes the process of integrating the various parts of the personality to become a whole person.

For Hughes, the poetic imagination can bring about healing to troubled minds and civilizations. The poet/shaman of today can effect healing through symbolic means, just as the shaman of the past could. By telling tales where people are symbolically changed, the poet becomes healer.

> Imagination is the faculty that enables us to locate and release the violated prisoner, or at least give her a voice. Those who are most successful in this we call poets. Initially the voice may well be embittered, resentful, destructive. It passes a harsh judgement on the poet, our representative. The punishment may be bloody, as in *The Bacchae* or *Gaudete*, terrifying, as in *King Lear* or 'The Ancient Mariner' or *Cave Birds*. But the pain and the fear, which may be real enough in some cases, are also symbolic of a process that is simultaneously destructive and creative, the breaking of the complacent, self-sufficient ego, which is the locus of guilt. Subsequently the voice becomes gentler and the healing process can begin.
>
> (Sagar, *The Laughter of Foxes*, p. 18)

The last poem chosen by Hughes for inclusion in *New Selected Poems 1957–1994* is 'A Dove'. While not being particularly profound, it has two doves, clattering through the trees in a wild and violent fashion, turning into 'Porpoises/Of dove-lust and blood splendour', riding 'Among flarings of mares and stallions', eventually ending up on a bough, 'wobbling top-heavy/ Into one and many'. The doves (and remember that doves pair for life) represent both order and disorder, but in the last line of the poem, they more or less keep their balance. They have achieved the kind of equilibrium that Hughes himself was continuing to seek through the processes of individuation and the healing power of the imagination.

Hughes believed in the idea of individuation.

THE USE OF MYTH

Hughes saw mythology as a means of getting closer to the Real by transcending the limitations of language. In myth, simple stories and the use of magical characters with special powers help a culture to come to terms with the Real. All civilizations have myths which use

archetypes, such as trickster birds, witches, courageous heroes and beautiful women to help explain and explore the lives we lead.

Myths seem to be essential to a people's cultural identity and are still very much in evidence today. The film *Star Wars* is perhaps an obvious example of a good versus evil scenario, with archetypal goodies and baddies. Its success shows how much our civilization craves its archetypes. The work of Angela Carter, too, demonstrates how deeply the imagery of fairy tale has become embedded in Western culture.

KEYWORD

Archetype: Literally a prototype from our ancient collective unconscious. Certain qualities such as bravery become embodied in character types which we all recognize. Hero figures are often archetypal in their birth, life story and characteristics. The clichéd use of archetype, without freshness or originality, becomes a stereotype.

KEY FACT

The Minotaur: In Greek mythology, a creature with a man's body and a bull's head. He lived in a labyrinth from which no one could escape. Every year the Minotaur was fed with seven young men and seven young women as tribute. Theseus succeeded in killing the Minotaur with the help of Ariadne, who gave him ball of string which led him back to the entrance of the labyrinth.

Seen in this light, the raven, the wolf and the owl are part of a collective consciousness. We recognize them because they have always been representations of the unknowable Real. We only have to allow our thoughts to dwell on the **Minotaur** of Crete, the wolf in 'Red Riding Hood', the ravens of Malta and the Tower of London, and the owls of enchanted forests or Harry Potter novels to recognize the power of symbols to affect our conscious and unconscious minds.

* * * *SUMMARY* * * *

Hughes's concerns are with:

- The power which lies behind the unconscious

- Man gone wrong

- The loss of the feminine principle in nature

- The healing power of the imagination

- Loss and lack

- The inadequacy of language

- The pursuit of the Real

- Myth as a way of getting closer to describing the Real.

5 Major Works: the Early Poetry

THE HAWK IN THE RAIN

Hughes's first collection, published in 1957, is a mix of different themes. There are some nature poems, observations of people, love poetry, philosophical observations and finally, some war poetry.

Very early in the collection can be found some of Hughes's most enduring work: famous poems such as 'The Jaguar', 'The Hawk in the Rain' and 'The Thought-Fox'. It was clear from the very start that Hughes was a prodigious new talent. W. S. Merwin, in one of the first reviews of the new collection, acknowledged him as an 'exciting new writer' (*New York Times*, 6 October 1957).

The animal world

The first poem in the collection, 'The Hawk in the Rain' (not in NSP, HIR p11), is a startling portent of what was to come in Hughes's later work. The language prepares us for the stark nihilism of *Crow* and the 'nature red in tooth and claw' backdrop to much of Hughes's work.

The hawk, who hangs 'effortlessly at height' is contrasted strongly with the poet, with his feet metaphorically stuck in clayey mud and almost drowned by a rain which 'hacks his head to the bone'. The hawk holds still against a raging wind, while the 'banging wind kills (these) stubborn hedges'. Hughes ponders on the chance of the hawk being caught out by a sudden change in wind direction and smashing into the ground, mixing his blood with 'the mire of the land'. The violence of the last line is startling even today, and seems like a manifesto of something new, seemingly anti-Romantic in feeling.

Animal imagery is present in many of the poems. There is 'The Jaguar' (NSP p. 4), observed by Hughes when he was a zoo attendant, 'on a short fierce fuse'. Other references to animals include: the macaw in

'Macaw and Little Miss' (not in *NSP*), 'bristling in a staring/ Combustion'; 'The Thought-Fox'(NSP p. 3), looked at earlier; The Horses (NSP p. 7) described as being 'Megalith-still'; and wolves. It can be instructive to comb the whole collection just to see how many references there are.

Love

The collection does have what passes for a tender love poem. 'September' (not in NSP) talks of sitting late, in the dark, exchanging kisses, time seemingly standing still. But even here, nothing stays the same and autumn is already at hand with the trees 'casting their crowns into the pools'. In 'Fallgrief's Girlfriends' (NSP p. 9), Fallgrief tries hard to see reason beyond intoxicating love, 'Where admirations giddy mannequin/ Leads every sense to motley'. He tries hard to seek a 'muck of a woman' to share his 'muck of existence', but in the end has to concede that:

> He has found a woman with such wit and looks
> He can brag of her in every company.

War

The last few poems take a wistful and melancholic view of war. There is the airman shot down, literally falling out of the sky, smashed to a pulp as he falls, but still probably alive in 'The Casualty' (NSP p. 15). He is burned and badly damaged but people drag him out and rest him against some sheaves of corn and 'arrange his limbs in order'. As onlookers press closer to take a look at the suffering man, his palm opens to reveal one of his eyes, staring up from a handkerchief. There is the soldier transfixed and terrified on his bayonet charge – 'Bayonet Charge' (NSP p. 16)), and the grieving woman – 'Griefs for Dead Soldiers' (not in NSP, HIR p. 54), having received her dreaded telegram, 'opening ... more terribly than any bomb', suffering her silent grief as men elsewhere bury their comrades in a mass grave, 'weighing their grief by the ounce, and burying it'. In 'Six Young Men' (NSP p. 17) a photograph holds in time the youth of the six soldiers, forty years after their deaths. Hughes recounts their senseless deaths before commenting that there's no man more alive today than they are, 'Nor prehistoric or fabulous beast more dead'.

Throughout these poems and others not mentioned, runs the symbol of the heart. The heart comes to symbolize not only life and love (or lack of both) but heroism. In 'The Ancient Heroes and the Bomber Pilot' (not in NSP, HIR p. 59), the pilot reflects on the bravery of chariot-fighting heroes of the Bronze Age whose wars were fought hand to hand and at great risk. He sees them as having greater hearts than his, even though he can destroy whole cities with a turn of his wrist.

The Martyrdom of Bishop Farrar

The man with the greatest heart is left till last. Bishop Farrar, placed on the stake at Carmarthen by Bloody Mary's men is reported to have said 'If I flinch from the pain of burning, believe not the doctrine I have preached'. Hughes writes a paean of praise to the bishop, ending in strong imagery which illustrates the heart and courage of the great man:

> ... while out of his eyes,
> Out of his mouth, fire like a glory broke,
> And smoke burned his sermons into the skies.

('The Martyrdom of Bishop Farrar', NSP p. 19)

The collection thus ends in high drama and with some fine rhyming poetry. The rhythms spring with great vigour while the rhymes give a sense of completeness.

The Hawk in the Rain is rather clumsy in its sentiments and perhaps over-worked in its ideas, but it still contains some powerful poetry and foreshadows all that was to come.

LUPERCAL

Lupercal (1960) has a different feel about it from *The Hawk in the Rain*. The subjects are varied and often begin in description or observation. The collection is less brash, more thoughtful and less bombastic. It is full of animals, among its other subjects, including horses, cats, a pig, a mouse, an otter, pike, a bullfrog and thrushes, and it explores them in a variety of ways.

Further explorations of the Real

The hawk in 'Hawk Roosting'(NSP p. 29) is a different sort of spirit to the one in 'Hawk in the Rain'. Firstly, the bird has become **personified**: he is no longer seen from a distance; he addresses us direct. He is in charge of all he surveys from his vantage point in a tall tree. He tells us it took the whole of Creation to produce each separate part of him, and 'Now I hold Creation in my foot'. He is a confident being. He sees himself as in control of his world, and tells us that he is 'going to keep things like this'. The **irony** of this is obvious to the reader, who knows that hawks have little control over their environment. At the same time, the hawk is a representative of Nature, who does. Hughes defended his hawk against some critics who accused it of being fascist 'the symbol of some horrible totalitarian genocide dictator'. He goes on to say that 'what I had in mind was that in this hawk, Nature is thinking' (Interview in *London Magazine*, January 1971, quoted in Sagar, *The Art of Ted Hughes*).

> ## KEYWORDS
>
> **Irony:** Where the reader perceives a discrepancy between words and meaning. Typically we say one thing when we mean another. A version of this occurs when a character does or says something which they interpret in one way, while the reader, knowing more than the character, can see things entirely differently. Usually, but not always, it is clear that the character is deluded.
>
> **Personification:** Where animals, objects, places or ideas are given human characteristics – turned into a character which thinks in human ways.

'The Bull Moses' (NSP p. 32) is a gentle, subservient giant as seen through the eyes of a boy. Here the animal is described from the outside, and although he is calm and unhurried, he still carries that profound depth which speaks of the Real: his blackness is 'depth/Beyond star', unfathomable. He has powers 'locked' and 'black'. The boy is careful to bolt the door of his stall.

Life and death

In 'View of a Pig' (NSP p. 34), the subject is a dead animal, deprived of power, a dead weight, 'too dead', 'a sack of wheat'. The poet suggests that 'Pigs must have hot blood'. In a sense, the dead pig is no longer a pig.

In the end, the boy can have no real feelings for it. Without life it is no longer dangerous, or a figure of fun. Here, language is being stretched, and a question posed: when is a pig not a pig?

'An Otter' (NSP p. 37) follows the same theme as 'View of a Pig': otters when alive are fluid, lithe, able to 'outfish fish', 'Of neither water nor land'. When captured by the hounds, the animal reverts to nothing at all except a pelt on the back of a chair. Sagar tells us that Hughes wrote the two parts separately. He laboured long and hard on the first part and was never fully satisfied with it. The second part 'virtually wrote itself' after a session of using the ouija board and a ouija spirit was responsible for the more spirit-like, reflective, tone (Sagar, *The Art of Ted Hughes*).

In another poem of childhood, the boy comes across a tramp, seemingly dead in a ditch in 'November' (NSP p. 36), 'The month of the drowned dog'. Running away from the tramp the boy enters a wood where he discovers the gamekeeper's spoils, hung out on a 'gibbet', some dry and lifeless, others much fresher and still dripping blood. Life and death are near cousins in this poem. This proximity is one of Hughes's preoccupations.

Other poems pick up similar themes. One might be forgiven for supposing that 'Mayday on Holderness' (p. 23) is not ostensibly about animals or the predator–prey story, but it is populated with animals such as crows, owls, stoats and seaworms. The River Humber sucks the life out of the land and the 'unkillable North Sea swallows it all'. The river becomes an alimentary canal sucking out a host of unpleasant substances, the by-products of Hull's endeavour. The supremely powerful forces of nature underlie Hughes's painterly 'Hull's sunset smudge' with something deeper and more powerful.

The most famous, and probably the most intense poem is 'Pike' (NSP p. 41), which we have already discussed (see p. 26). It is the clearest expression in the collection of the inexpressible 'Real', and the tension which exists on the thin line between life and death.

The final poem in the collection is 'Lupercal' itself. Here we find a standard Hughes device: the recycling of an ancient myth to suit new purposes. It is based on the Roman fertility festival for barren women, called Lupercalia, which was celebrated on 15 February. First goats and dogs were slaughtered in sacrifice. Then young men, smeared in blood and milk, ran through the streets hitting the barren women with goatskin whips. The poem works from the perspective of the dog, the women, the goats and the racers. As an exercise you might like to try seeing how this final poem sums up the themes of the book and tries to resolve some of them.

CROW

Unfinished work

Crow was to have been a fully fledged working of a modern myth. Hughes spent many years collecting material for it and had a fully visualized story to which he was working. In 1969, after Plath's death, he stopped and felt unable to finish the project. He had, however, enough poems to produce a collection and *Crow* was published in 1970. It may be that Hughes was not thinking very clearly, for although the collection caused a huge amount of interest when it was published, he came to regret not giving his readers any kind of context in which to place *The Life and Songs of the Crow*.

Everything sings its own song

The story was to have been largely prose but scattered with songs and poems, both from Crow and others. Everything he came across could have a song or a dialogue with him, adding to his store of knowledge and helping to assuage his curiosity. In Keith Sagar's words, 'Every plant, stone, creature, has its own version of any event. Everything sings its own song about itself' (Sagar, *The Laughter of Foxes*, p. 175).

Even without a context, the poems in *Crow* were strong and seemed to speak to their time. The main character, Crow himself, was an engaging chap who seemed often to be working in the dark. His quest for the source of Creation, and for eternal happiness, mirrored that of his readership. Besides this, Crow had a healthy disregard for God, a flawed personage who himself seemed to have lost his way. In times where the Church of England seemed lost, and where in jokes, if not in reality, it seemed possible for bishops not to believe in God, *Crow* struck a chord.

The Crow myth

Hughes often tried to make up for his mistake by explaining bits of the Crow myth in readings, essays, articles, or in letters to friends, but it was left to his close friend Keith Sagar to put the whole thing together. The full myth is too long to tell here and is fully described in Sagar's appendix to *The Laughter of Foxes*.

In brief:

God has terrible nightmares about a hand which comes to throttle him. The hand becomes a voice and abuses God's greatest creation – mankind.

A representative of Man arrives at the Gate of Heaven, demanding that God take life back because men no longer want it. God is so angry that he challenges the Voice to do better with the same materials and sends Man back to Earth.

The upshot of this is that Crow is born, literally through a womb.

As he goes through his life, various ordeals, trials and experiences shape him into what he becomes: a crow, just like a man.

God arrives to see how Crow is getting on. Crow tries to help God but his efforts usually go wrong, and the more God tries to oppose him, the stronger and more crow-like (man-like) he becomes.

As Crow learns about Creation, he learns most significantly about pain, or what Hughes calls 'travail'. Like a child, Crow is on a long journey of self-discovery.

Crow eventually meets an Eskimo spirit guide. The guide gives Crow a set of songs, each song bestowing a magic power.

Crow comes to a river which he must cross to reach the Happy Land. He meets an ugly hag who insists that he carry her across the river. On the way she asks him questions: if he gets the answers correct she becomes lighter. When Crow gets all the answer correct, the hag turns into a beautiful and naked maiden, and they both run off towards an oak wood. *Crow* can thus be seen to be a myth of individuation.

The poems in *Crow* barely get beyond the first half of the story. The Crow character turns up again in various guises, most notably in *Cave Birds*, but the heroic Crow epic itself was at an end.

Simultaneous song

The mythic quality of *Crow* is strengthened by the universe created for it. The earth of this myth is dark, like a literary version of **film noir**. It is almost as if Crow's explorations shine a torch beam at one thing at a time, illuminating it for an instant before returning it to darkness.

Crow's world does not follow Western civilization's concept of linear time: its version of cause and effect is not so clear-cut. All of creation is happening at the same time and 'all the episodes of history are present, as in all the different rooms of a gigantic hotel, and every single thing goes on happening for the first time forever' (Sagar, op. cit. p. 174).

> **KEYWORD**
>
> Film noir: Is a stylistic device in film or television which uses dark, brooding, atmospheric lighting effects to increase a sense of danger, or the pervasion of evil forces. Recent examples include Ridley Scott's *Bladerunner* and many scenes in *The X-Files*.

So Crow can be present at all events in Earth's history and can hop between them at will. All man's triumphs and disasters are available for scrutiny and comment. There are links to ancient cultures in this view of the world; the Australian aboriginal concept of the Dreamtime (very fashionable when Hughes was writing) is an obvious example.

Crow found the world bemusing.

The Trickster

Hughes had a lifelong fascination with the crow figure. Crows and ravens are found in the myths of many (if not all) cultures in the world. Their most obvious association is with death, partly because they are usually the first to arrive after a battle, taking carrion, particularly the eyes. Their blackness has also been linked with dark forces and they are often seen as harbingers of death. For example, Shakespeare's Lady Macbeth says 'The raven itself is hoarse,/ That croaks the fatal entrance of Duncan/ Under my battlements' (*Macbeth*, Act 1 scene 5).

The raven and crow are indistinguishable in myth and fable. They are not always seen as birds of ill omen. Some cultures characterize them as tricksters and some even allow them positive magical powers. The native culture of the north-west coast of America has the raven in the roles of mischief-maker, trickster and saviour. It is often through mischief that ravens bring about good in the stories.

Hughes's Crow is rather unsure of himself, despite being a cocky individual with a penchant for trying to be the people's saviour. His efforts are usually less than helpful, as can be seen in 'A Childish Prank' (NSP p. 91). In his early days on Earth he tries to help God out with his dilemma about how to give life to Adam and Eve. Here Hughes taps into at least two legends, that of the Bible and the **Talmud**.

KEYWORD

Talmud: The collection of Jewish religious and civil law. It contains moral doctrine and ritual based on the Scriptures. Second only to the Bible in Jewish religious life.

Crow does not hang about and goes straight to the heart of the problem by biting the worm in two and stuffing 'into man the tail half/ With the wounded end hanging out', and the head end into woman until it creeps up 'To peer out through her eyes/ Calling its tail-half to join up quickly, quickly.'

The same over-reaction happens in 'Crow's First Lesson' (NSP p. 92) where love and lust get accidentally but permanently linked. We know that Crow must be learning because he 'flies guiltily off'. The other poems in the collection explore further the quest that Crow is on, and that humans are on, the search for meaning and, more importantly, the search for identity and purpose.

Crow was a powerful and coherent vision, sadly not fully realized. But even in its unfinished state, the collection sets up a fascinating imaginative universe, and gives the world a new character, a character born again out of old myths and given new relevance through the growing environmental movement of the 1970s and in a (Western) world which tried to protect itself by using a concept called MAD –

Mutually Assured Destruction (through joint nuclear attack). Part of the story of the late twentieth century was that of man's quest to avoid extinction and find better ways of relating to nature. *Crow* is Hughes's contribution to the debate.

✴ ✴ ✴ *SUMMARY* ✴ ✴ ✴

In Hughes's early work:

● The content is a little patchy but shows a poet moving toward a set of themes and a unique vision

● We already see him exploring the inexpressible, unknowable powers that lie beyond the fabric of our lives

● Unfeeling Nature as expressed through animals is very important

● He began to use myths and legends as powerful devices and sources of inspiration.

Major Works: Post-*Crow*

6

GAUDETE

The framing story

Perhaps conscious of his mistake in not making clear the framing 'story' of *Crow*, Hughes was keen to give a summary of *Gaudete* at the front of a collection in a piece called 'Argument'. An Anglican clergyman is abducted by spirits and replaced by a duplicate. The substitute takes an individual approach to his new ministry until his powers are taken away and the original (changed) minister is returned.

The notion of *Gaudete* is that the dualities of life, good/bad, light/dark, heaven/hell, are part of a whole. The one is balanced by the other. The collection is prefaced by two quotations, one from the Greek philosopher Heraclitus stating that **Hades** and **Dionysos** are one being; the other being from *Parzival*, Book xv, which again speaks of two men being one, of two sons being of one man:

> One could say that 'they' were fighting in this way if one were to speak of two. These two were one, for 'my brother and I' is one body, like good man and good wife.

KEY FACT

Dionysos: God of wine and mystic ecstasy. He had great powers and rescued Ariadne from Hades.

Hades: God of the dead. He ruled over the Underworld and would let no-one return to the living.

After the 'Argument', comes a 'Prologue' which introduces us to the Reverend Lumb and his descent into an apocalyptic underworld. Here he encounters horrific images: mass graves in the street, a dead man walking, a woman half alive, half dead whom he cannot help. As his nightmare journey continues he is flogged to unconsciousness, becoming a **tree**, and the tree is then flogged into life. In Graves's *The White Goddess* we find a reference to a Naked King crucified on a lopped oak. Dancers surround him chanting 'Kill! kill! kill!' and 'Blood! blood! blood!' The king is the shaman.

The tree becomes the substitute Lumb who is then forced to shoot a white sacrificial bull. The scene becomes a slaughterhouse, Lumb finds himself beneath the white bull as it is winched overhead; its belly is cut and he is drenched under half a ton of guts and blood. Eventually, as if in birth, he manages to escape and find some stone steps which he hopes will lead back to the world he recently left. The 'real' Lumb emerges in a lake in Western Island and leaves a notebook of poems with three girls who take them to their priest. These poems form the final section of the book.

Gaudete is Latin for 'rejoice' and refers to the birth of the Saviour. In this case, any birth must be seen as ironic – Lumb is nobody's saviour.

In the main narrative, Lumb is portrayed as a man with a deep unconscious that is represented by the spirit world, and which operates at the same time as his conscious mind. He interacts with the world, abuses it, and then contemplates his actions to try to make sense of them.

Narrative structure

It may sound strange to describe a poetry collection in terms of narrative structure but, like *Crow* and, later, *Cave Birds*, the main sequence in *Gaudete* has a strong sense of story. In some ways, it reads much more like a novel although each episode or characterization is contained in a poetic structure which often becomes prose-like.

By using this device, Hughes introduces rhythms, tensions and climaxes which slowly build through the main section. It would be pointless to take any one of the poems out of context and study it separately because it is part of a whole. This is reinforced by the fact that Hughes chose only poems from the Epilogue for inclusion in his *New Selected Poems*.

Accessible language

The language of *Gaudete* is much more accessible than *Crow*, although, as we have seen, the imagery can sometimes be more violent and disturbing. An example chosen at random will suffice to demonstrate the flat style:

> Now she can look at the birds,
> Her father's prisoners,
> Her girlhood's confidantes.
> She sees just how squalid and miserable they are.
> And they regard her without any affection.

(GD p. 45)

Here the language is matter-of-fact, almost anti-poetic. This style is something that Hughes continued to experiment with, alternating it with the much denser style of *Crow* and *Cave Birds* and bringing it to a mature fruition in such works as *Moortown Diary* and *Birthday Letters*. Hughes used different language styles for different subjects and effects. We must remember that though his collections were published separately, the poems in them were being written at different times and often simultaneously.

Gaudete began life as the scenario for a film script and this can be seen in its episodic quality and in the sharpness of its scenes and incidents. The language is very cinematic in places, as if describing in words the effects that film can create. At times, it almost sounds like an instruction to a camera operator:

> He sees a fish rise
> Off the point of the long broken finger of boulders
> Which pokes out from the lake, from the island.
> The lake is oil-still
> As if it were pressed flat
>
> (GD p. 77)

The effect of the language throughout the book is to present us with a series of episodic scenes which build, just as a film builds, intercutting different but connected lives in the mesmerizing way that film can do.

The final section, the 'Epilogue', becomes much more formally poetic, with mostly short lines and verses. The language becomes more compressed and convoluted and the themes of *Crow*, birth, death, despair and confusion, begin to reassert themselves, but this time through a first person 'I'. They constitute an inner monologue, poured onto the paper by a man who has been on a quest for himself, 'seeking control and decision' as outlined in the 'Prologue'.

Subject matter

After the strong unpalatable images of the 'Prologue', the main section of the book covers seemingly banal lives and everyday activities. A series of country people follow interconnected lives doing ordinary things: a veritable soap opera of peeling potatoes, going for walks, hunting, shooting and fishing. Eventually, the hidden life of the village becomes clear as we discover an excessive amount of extramarital dallying and the application of gun law for good measure. There is a suicide. We learn that Lumb has seduced most of the village women and has set up a coven of witches in the church where he is the all-powerful Master, assisted by his housekeeper Maud, a practising witch. He is eventually hunted to death by men before being burned, along with two of his parishioners. The horror of the piece partly comes from being offset against the mundane. As if to accentuate the banality of life on the surface, the Reverend Lumb's presence is always announced by his blue van, parked outside a home or in a wood.

The world of *Gaudete* is very tangible, and redolent of Hughes's own country life. At one level, it begins as an everyday story of country folk but soon becomes a dark tale where the priest becomes satanic, the women try to recover their control over the world by joining Lumb's coven, and the men are powerless in the face of what happens, voyeuristic (they are seen watching what goes on, often through binoculars), and eventually brutal and violent.

The collection is also of its time, written in the 1970s when a lot of films based on literature had begun to explore the Real in both country (for example, *Straw Dogs*, 1971) and town (*A Clockwork Orange*, 1971). The senseless nature of violence, unexplained and uncontrollable, was a motif of the time, and was a reminder to those observing it that the destiny of human lives is not controlled or controllable. The story is also one concerned with individuation and rebirth, the hope that through adversity, man shall find a newer, purer, perhaps more harmonious existence.

CAVE BIRDS
Crow was, if nothing else, an experiment with language, and Hughes continued the experiment in *Cave Birds*, perhaps his most difficult collection of poems. The collection is subtitled 'An Alchemical Cave Drama', which alerts us at once to the fact that there is a unifying theme for the work. Alchemists believed they could transmute base metals into gold, and one form of alchemy could be to turn the base metal of man into metaphorical gold – to redeem man and set him out on the right path. The collection tells the story of a trial and stands as a metaphor for the trials of man, and perhaps in particular of Ted Hughes.

There are shifts of viewpoint in this collection and there is often an 'I', a 'narrator' or observer, who is much closer to the action than the omniscient narrator of *Crow*. At other times, the viewpoint is simply that of observer, and the narrator does nothing but describe events without the rhetorical and ironic spin of *Crow*.

The collection might be thought as an inner quest, a searching for an integration of the self. The persona in the poems goes through a series of dramas, often presided over by authority figures who are named in the titles of some of the poems, The Summoner, The Interrogator, The Judge, The Executioner, The Knight, The Gatekeeper, The Baptist, which in themselves tell a story. Then there are The Plaintiff, The Accused and The Scapegoat. Eventually a woman figure emerges in 'A Green Mother' (TB p. 87). Hughes, in the midst of what appears to be a fragmented and difficult series of poems, introduces the balm of the feminine principle and she offers the protagonist 'a busy hive of heavens' from which to choose on earth. The multitudinous heavens offered are built around the flora and fauna of the world and are described in terms of the Garden of Eden. Intellectual and religious heavens are also offered and the Green Mother says she will act as a guide to these too. The poem is comforting, composed of gentle words and healing images.

> … It is heaven's mother
> The grave is her breast, her nipple in its dark aura.
> Her milk is unending life.

As the sequence of poems develops, we begin to feel the force for integration and to get a sense of an individual, born fragmented and confused, slowly being brought to a state of oneness. The feminine principle seems to be crucial to the process, and can be seen in such poems as 'A Riddle', (TB p. 90) 'I shall deliver you … My firstborn … To Cry'; 'After There was Nothing Came a Woman' (TB p. 93); and in 'Bride and Groom Lie Hidden for Three Days' (TB p. 97, NSP p. 127) where, ostensibly at least, a man and a woman appear to be assembling each other.

Bride and Groom
'Bride and Groom Lie Hidden for Three Days' is worth further study. You may care to examine the sensuality and sexuality of the piece, heightened by the loving care with which both parties assemble each

other and join together. The last line, 'They bring each other to perfection', is a description of the sexual and spiritual act, but also of the integration of separate elements into a whole. Then there is the imagery of the body compared with the harsher language of the earlier poems in the *Cave Birds* collection.

Rebirth and integration

Finally, man becomes reborn in 'The Owl Flower' (TB p. 99), a bit like the hawk of 'Hawk Roosting', but not so sure of himself. He is a staggering thing, 'Fired with rainbows', and, like Crow, who 'Trembled featherless elbows in the nest's filth,' The Owl Flower 'Blinks at source'. In the next poem, 'The Risen' (TB p. 100, NSP p. 128), we see a slightly less certain persona than Crow, still able to fly, still able to impress:

> When he soars, his shape
>
> Is a cross, eaten by light,
> On the Creator's face

He is now a Christ-like figure. This time round, however, there is the possibility that he might be tamed to man's desires for

> ... when will he land
> On a man's wrist?

The 'Finale' rams home the message that even at the end of man's struggle to rid himself of all that he despises about himself, there is still a point of doubt about his happiness: even in the final act of rebirth and atonement, 'up comes a goblin'.

MOORTOWN DIARY

In some ways, this collection seems out of step with the some of Hughes's more structured and complex works. It is firmly based in Hughes's farming experiences. In his preface, he calls the poems, rather disingenuously, 'improvised verses', describing them as if he just threw them off without thought. He then goes on to call them 'journal notes'. He also describes them as attempts to catch the moment, to try to make a snapshot of an event or experience before 'the processes of "memory", the poetic process had already started'. As he later shows, he had to make some attempt at 'translation' before releasing the poems, but 'Altering any word felt like retouching an old home movie with new bits of fake-original voice and fake-original actions.'

This turns the collection into an examination of memory and the poetic process. It begs questions about what the poet does to remembered experience, and what poetic technique does to the veracity of memory. One of the major questions in the study of autobiography is how much memory is distorted after the event by the addition of material, denial, the reshaping of events, false memory and family myth. *Moortown Diary* is another way of examining this question. We can ask, among other things, how close Hughes has got to the 'truth' by trying to keep himself out of the poems and letting events tell their own story.

In the preface he explains how an ancient way of life had been preserved in the isolated Devon valleys, and how he felt that he had seen this way of life before it was changed for ever by modern farming practices. He describes the effects of these practices in harsh terms: 'the product itself had become a weirdly scandalous unwanted surplus, the livestock a danger to public health … the very soil a kind of poison, the rivers sewers.'. Here we hear strong echoes of Rachel Carson's clarion call of the 1960s, *Silent Spring*, which awakened activists to the real threat of global catastrophe if farming practices and technology were not kept in check or reversed.

The poems do have a 'rough' quality about them, in the sense that we feel the elements at work, and we are led to understand the relationship of man and beast, and man and nature, through the day-to-day workings of farm life. In this world, bulls are dehorned; there are foxhunts, 'a cloud of excitements'; ewes have their lambs in the unnatural 'comfort' of the barn, or mourn dead twins; and farmers joke about 'bloody great hands'.

2 May 1972

Got up!
Went to farm.
Came home.
Had some tea
Wrote Poem

3 May 1972

Hughes tried to tell farming life just as it was.

Through it all we are aware of Hughes's environmental themes. It is as if, even when not consciously fashioning 'poetry', Hughes is still an active filter on the world. He cannot disengage his sensibilities. A look at 'Tractor' (NSP p. 179) will demonstrate this. One would imagine that Hughes would see the tractor as a symbol of technological progress, a destroyer of an ancient way of life, but instead the tractor becomes like the other beasts of the farm in its intransigence and latent power. When it has jabbered 'Into happy life' it becomes animal-like, 'steaming with sweat,/ Raging and trembling and rejoicing'. It becomes a mechanical manifestation of the Real,

> Like a demon demonstrating
> A more-than-usually-complete materialization –

Unusually for Hughes, he personifies the machine, making it mock the farmer, ridiculing him as he tries to start it. By doing this, he shows us our own propensity for personifying animals and inanimate objects, as our way of dealing with life when it doesn't go as planned. Today we ascribe malice to computers which 'lose' our files or in other ways reflect our stupidity. Mankind has always ironically blamed those things which show us our frailty. In the case of the farmer trying to start his tractor, the personification represents his projections onto a world where the intractable, the Real, are inexpressible in any other terms. Humans cannot control the Real so they are forced to find other ways of dealing with it.

In direct contrast to the tractor is the tender scene of Hughes teaching a newborn calf to suckle from its mother in 'Teaching a Dumb Calf' (MD p. 45). Anyone who as ever done this will recognize the calf, who 'was trying to suck but lacked the savvy' until success is achieved and we are left with the satisfying tableau 'the happy warm peace' of new mother and offspring. Here, the mother is at first intransigent, lashing out at farmer and calf, but is eventually helped back to suckling motherhood by the persistence and patience of the farmer. Man works with nature to achieve a desired result.

The final poem in the sequence, 'Hands', is an elegy to Hughes's father-in-law Jack Orchard. Jack's hands had been his major tools throughout his life, and the poem chronicles his use of them, 'Hands more of a piece with your tractor/ Than with your own nerves'. As the poem concludes, his hands, folded in death, become slender and white, like his mother's, 'Your mother's hands suddenly in your hands – / In that final strangeness of elegance.'

In those last two lines, Hughes reminds us of the cycles of birth and death, of our inheritance of the past, of the continuity of nature and of our own mortality. The farmer's death comes also to symbolize the death of a friendship and the end of the ancient way of life which Hughes outlines in the Preface.

THE LAUREATE POEMS

Ted Hughes succeeded Sir John Betjeman as Poet Laureate in 1984. It seemed to many to be a strange choice, following as it did on the poet of suburbia, who seemed steeped in the cosy world of the English middle class. For some, Betjeman defined a certain sort of Englishness, following in the footsteps of such 'English' poets as William Wordsworth, Alfred Lord Tennyson and John Masefield. As it turned out, Hughes's Laureate work put him in a direct line of English (British) poets. Hughes always kept his work strongly based in his own sense of self and belonging.

Poets Laureate are not asked to commemorate specific events; their role is to respond as they feel appropriate at any given time. Hughes did not duck these responsibilities and wrote seven pieces or collections of pieces in his time as Poet Laureate. The poems are collected in *Rain-Charm for the Duchy*, and show how he could express his main themes through interaction with the notion of monarchy and what it stands for. In an epigraph to the book, Hughes expresses the view that the soul of a nation is linked with the Crown 'to keep it whole'.

The title poem, (NSP p. 285, RCD p. 1) was written in response to the christening of HRH Prince Harry. It is set in the duchy of the title. This is not the true Duchy of Cornwall but an imaginative construct which takes in most of the watersheds of Devon's rivers. Its origin is in Hughes's love of salmon fishing. In a note to 'Rain-Charm for the Duchy' (RCD p. 51), he explains how in drought years salmon find it very difficult to get up river to spawn and occasionally have to 'rush' the low rivers in a squirming, seething mass bid for survival. Written in 1984, a drought year, 'Rain-Charm for the Duchy' records a spectacular torrential rainstorm and the deluge of water as the storm breaks: 'Rain didn't so much fall as collapse'. This is a deluge of the same magnitude as that in 'The Hawk in the Rain', and it wakens all the rivers so that the waiting salmon, 'deep in thunder', begin to move. As the rain gives life to the rivers, so the Duchy of Cornwall itself gives life to land it covers.

The waters break, linking the rain with birth, and they drench the land, thus symbolizing christening. The salmon, like sperm, all have one aim in life, to reach the head of the stream and complete the natural process of procreation. Running closely with these fundamental themes is an echo of ecological concerns: the River Okement is full of detergent bottles and Pepsi Cola cans. Each river is characterized by its main associations; the Dart has bareback ponies, the Tamar carries its ancient legends of 'rusty knights' and the Tavy rinses out her 'stale mouth' tasting of tin and copper.

The poem celebrates new life and new beginnings while emphasizing the continuing cycle of regeneration. It is one of Hughes's most affirmative poems.

In the 'Dream of the Lion', a poem on the eighty-fifth birthday of the Queen Mother, Hughes sets out a very English landscape: 'an ancient land. The Land of the Lion'. In it, he evokes images of England in myth, the lion and the unicorn being strong symbols of monarchy. For Queen Elizabeth's sixtieth birthday, Hughes evokes a new nativity, with three angels bringing the Queen, and therefore the kingdom, three gifts; those of water, the spirit of earth (the Way) and blood.

A vision of Britain

The Laureate poems have proved a problem area for both reviewers and academics. Discussion centres around whether or not Hughes is being ironic and subverting the office, whether the poems are any good, and whether he is being sycophantic. Neil Roberts, for example, in an article in *Critical Quarterly*, (vol. 27, no.2, summer 1985, p. 3), sees an ironic overstatement in the drenching storm of 'Rain-Charm for the Duchy' and the christening of Prince Harry which it celebrates. Others have tried to detect a certain laughing behind the hand, but there is little evidence to show that this is the case. The epigraph at the front of the collection makes clear Hughes's belief that the Crown is at the hub of the nation, and his notes on the poems clearly indicate that he is trying to explore 'a boyhood fanatic patriotism' (RCD p. 53).

What is most interesting perhaps is how Hughes is thrown back on describing nature and his feelings towards it, as he follows the rather forced brief of a Poet Laureate. We sense that he is not fully sure of the role of the monarchy, and his poems reflect the growing drift in purpose. In 'A Birthday Masque for Her Majesty Queen Elizabeth II's Sixtieth Birthday' he speaks directly of the need for a new collective vision:

> a melt of strange metals.
> To be folded and hammered,
> Re-folded, re-hammered.

> (RCD p. 16)

The poem ends with the line 'The ring of people', a reference to Black Elk, a Sioux shaman, who, in a vision, saw the 'ring' of his people, the symbol of their unity, destroyed. Hughes's message, that Britain is a great melting pot of cultures and history which needs to be reinvented, is perhaps the strongest in the Laureate poems.

The collection reads like a snapshot of an England still caught looking back to the days of Albion, the days of myth and legend when the Lion and the Unicorn ruled the spiritual and cultural landscape, when legends as old as Arthur and older kept the people in good heart. The monarchy for Hughes comes to symbolize continuity in this collective culture. In 'A Unicorn called Ariel', the unicorn (symbol for the current queen and also for the monarchy as a whole) comes through from the past. The last verse states that 'The Unicorn can only win/ The race she was born to run.' This rather sycophantic but heart-felt statement of continuity perhaps indicates a man more at ease with himself at the end of his life.

Hughes is a poet in the English tradition.

* * * *SUMMARY* * * *

Hughes's post-*Crow* poetry:

- Demonstrates a development of his major themes

- Uses both mythic and 'real' landscapes to express those themes

- Uses a variety of styles and language

- Displays a strong use of narrative

- Becomes less fatalistic.

Major Works: *Birthday Letters*

7

In 1998, near the end of his life, Hughes decided to publish a remarkable book. It contained his thoughts and feelings about his relationship with Sylvia Plath, and became as close to **confessional writing** as he was ever likely to get. The collection went on to win the Whitbread Book of the Year and the T. S. Eliot prize.

> ## KEYWORD
>
> Confessional writing: Poetry or prose where the subject is subjective and personal. The work of Robert Lowell and some of his American contemporaries became known as 'confessional poetry' and Sylvia Plath wrote many confessional poems.

PUTTING THE RECORD STRAIGHT?

Hughes always maintained that his silence was in order to protect his children, although he was an intensely private man anyway, and someone who also wished to protect the memory (his memory) of Plath. There is no doubt that the barrage of criticism aimed at him caused much pain. His daughter Frieda affirms that 'He never spoke publicly about what happened ... so everybody made it up. That was very difficult. He told me he should have said something, that he regretted remaining silent,' (Frieda Hughes, 'In the Name of my Father', *Daily Mail Weekend*, 3 November 2001).

The poems in the collection were written over a long period beginning after Plath's death. Some had been published earlier in various places but most were revealed to the public for the first time. All but two of the poems are addressed directly to Plath, or at least a persona who stands for Plath in Hughes's eyes. The 'you' in the poems is a construct to allow Hughes to express his own feelings. There can be no possibility of a reply. In this sense, the poems are a way for Hughes to work out and record his feelings.

The collection is a chronological account of a love story carried on beyond the death of one of its subjects. The chronology gives the collection the flavour of a story being told. The 'letters' are in the form of poems mainly addressed to Plath, usually alluding to her own poems or interweaving with them. The tone is reflective and the book charts the tempestuous nature of their marriage.

HUGHES OBSESSED BY HIS DEAD WIFE

In many ways *Birthday Letters* demonstrates a striking similarity to Thomas Hardy's *Poems 1912–1916*. Hardy, another intensely private man, wrote his love poems after the death of his wife Emma to whom he had been unhappily married. Hardy went back to the early happy days of his life with Emma, ceaselessly going over the same ground in an attempt to capture what had been there. Hughes, too, was forced back to discover what was really there in his own first marriage, and he too obsesses over what he regarded as the main love of his life.

Birthday Letters is basically the record of a tragedy, or one man's attempt to come to terms with it. The imagery is of a man in a dream, of sleepwalking, of the labyrinth, of people taking parts in a play they do not understand and cannot control. Drowning and burning are common elements, as is blood.

There is a medieval sense of being entrapped in a world of someone else's making, of following a path which feels as if it is licensed by free will but which, in fact, is acting out a predestined pattern:

> That day the solar system married us
> Whether we knew it or not.
>
> ('St Botolph's', BL p. 14)

THEMES

Holocaust

The Hughes–Plath relationship was overshadowed by Plath's father, whose death when she was only eight was to have a profound effect on both herself and Ted. Her mother had not allowed her to grieve. Sylvia felt resentment and fascination, turning the daddy, the betraying male, into Ted as the current version of this powerful, seductive, destructive force acting on her. Her most powerful poem about her father, 'Daddy', seethes with anger and Nazi Holocaust imagery. It is an example of the sort of poem that Hughes was encouraging Plath to write – a bright fire of images and emotion which they both hoped would exorcize the demons of her earlier life and thus set the way for growth. Written at the time of Ted's affair with Assia Wevill, it also parallels her intense pain at that relationship, claiming that 'Every woman adores a Fascist,/ The boot in the face, the brute/ Brute heart of a brute like you.' Far from assuaging the fire, the technique seemed to be fuelling it. In 'The God' (p. 190), Hughes explores this, touching on 'Flames I had lit unwitting/ That whitened in the oxygen jet/ Of your incantatory whisper'.

BURNING UP

Sagar points out that behind all the imagery, particularly in Plath's poems, lie two similar myths, that of **Phaeton** and **Icarus**. Both Plath and Hughes had a 'burning' desire to strip away the false self but 'The process of burning away the false self and verse gets out of hand, becomes a holocaust… In the myth they were enacting, Hughes's role was that of alchemist/midwife'. (Sagar, *The Laughter of Foxes*, p. 79).

Ariel, Phaeton and Icarus

Hughes and Plath created their own myth when they were together. It was part of their feeling that they were different and was a way of feeding their creativity. The basis of this was the story of *The Tempest*, Plath taking the role of **Ariel** and Hughes that of Prospero, the rescuer and redeemer. The relationship between Plath and Hughes, and that between Plath and her poetry, are caught up in this mythology. Hughes had assumed that Plath's poetic and psychological fires would be controlled and turned into positive energy under his direction. Plath saw Hughes as a magician, who could control elemental forces. Much of the imagery in *Birthday Letters* bears out Hughes's view of how things went terribly wrong and out of control as she burned up. In 'Fairy Tale' (BL p. 159) Hughes describes her Ogre (her dead father and thus her psychological destroyer) glowing in the dark 'like a volcano'. The intense heat is captured in lines such as:

> ... I never saw
> His effigy there, burning in your tears
> Like a thing of tar.

KEY FACTS

Ariel: One of the seven angelic princes in Heywood's *Hierarchy of the Blessed Angels* (1635). Crops up in various guises including one of the rebel angels in Milton's *Paradise Lost*, but most notably in Shakespeare's *The Tempest*. In this version, Ariel is imprisoned in a split tree for twelve years by the witch Sycorax for being unable to perform tasks beyond his powers. Eventually Ariel becomes the slave of Caliban, who cruelly misuses him until Prospero frees him.

Icarus: Flew from Crete with his father Daedalus using wings made from feathers held together by wax. Icarus flew too close to the sun, the wax melted and Icarus fell to his doom in the sea.

Phaeton: Son of Helios the sun god. He took his father's fiery chariot and, losing control, created mayhem, nearly setting fire to the whole world before destroying himself.

Later in his life, Hughes returned to a myth he felt was more apt for his story: the Orpheus story in which Orpheus goes down into the underworld to regain his dead wife Euridice. In his final work, *Alcestis*, Hughes took the Orpheus legend and transformed it into the story of Admetus, who has sacrificed his wife Alcestis (in place of himself), and feels remorse for not having valued his happiness with her. Admetus goes into the underworld, but this time his pain and suffering are deemed so great that he has paid his debt, and Alcestis is returned to him. As Sagar points out: 'Hughes finally distils this positive vision. The last line of his last work is 'let this give man hope' (op. cit. p. 86).

HEAT OF PASSION

Other people creep into the story of *Birthday Letters*, including Assia Wevil, who is powerfully described in 'Dreamers'. Here, he describes, in terms of a fairy tale, that she was a 'Black Forest wolf, a witches' daughter/ Out of Grimm'. He sees her through Plath's eyes, emphasizing dark Germanic undertones. There are echoes again of the

Like the rest of us Hughes found it difficult to control his life.

Nazi Holocaust imagery of 'Daddy'. Apart from his view of Plath's mental state, he accurately describes the daydream-like quality of his falling in love with someone new. In this, Hughes achieves something very difficult: to be inside two people's thoughts simultaneously in one poem.

THE UNRELIABILITY OF MEMORY AND VIEWPOINT

The poems often revolve around a lack of certainty. Hughes is very conscious that his memory is fallible and his viewpoint distorted. As you read the poems you will find a theme of questioning events. In 'The Rabbit Catcher', he tries to remember the source of a quarrel, 'How had it started?' The first two poems in the book begin with questions: 'Where was it, in the Strand?' (Fulbright Scholars), and 'What were those Caryatids bearing?' ('Caryatids' p. 4). Although a useful reflective device, it serves the much greater purpose of reminding us of the fallibility of memory. There is an acknowledgement that the facts (and therefore the viewpoint of the writer) are not certain.

The somewhat strident and assertive viewpoint which can be detected in the poems is ameliorated by the uncertainty and by the very fact that one voice (Hughes) is telling the story. We can be certain that although there is an effort to be true to the memory of things, the strong voice reminds us that what we are reading is a personal and therefore subjective account. In 'Your Paris' (BL p. 36) and 'You Hated Spain', (BL p. 39, NSP p. 294) we can see this principle at work.

In 'Your Paris' Hughes emphasizes the differences between her view of Paris and his. She, he says, has American sensibilities, and sees the war-torn city in terms of Impressionist paintings, and through the eyes of American fiction. Hughes, by contrast, claims to see Paris as a 'post-war utility survivor' where the ghosts of occupation walk the streets. In the early poems we see the emerging chasms between the newly-weds which are not apparent (or significant) to them at the time.

In 'You Hated Spain', the differences are highlighted again, for Hughes says that Spain frightens her while he feels at home. Spain epitomized all that Hughes was obsessed with, 'The blood-raw light', bullfights, 'the African black edges to everything'. She hates the 'Watching bulls awkwardly butchered'. It is not the Spain of her imaginings. He characterizes her reaction as the innocent abroad 'thinking it is still your honeymoon'. Ominously, he finishes with her being 'Happy, and all your poems still to be found' – and all their troubles still be discovered.

Such views might seem a little simplistic, almost glib, but Hughes is not so much explaining, or even apologizing, as trying to show the events as he sees (remembers) them. His view must by definition be one-sided and partisan. It is the lack of an absolute voice in *Birthday Letters* which gives it much of its force. Here is a man saying what he feels – expressing privately (originally) his deep and troubled relationship with Plath and showing his feelings in a warm and loving way.

FATALISM

Beyond all this is the notion of fate: a force moving to confound the best-made plans. The natural consequence of all this is that even poets, even the shaman that Hughes felt himself to be, are subject in the end to what we earlier referred to as the Real. *Birthday Letters* is a testament to the fatalism that marked Hughes's work and shows how it works on a very human scale. A telling moment from 'The Owl' (p. 33) illustrates the sudden unexpectedness of life: the persona, Hughes, is showing off to Plath in a boyish way by whistling the call of a distressed rabbit. Suddenly a tawny owl swoops down, 'splaying its pinions/ Into my face, taking me for a post'.

LANGUAGE

This collection of love poems is tender and affectionate but certainly not sloppy or sentimental. The language used is similar to that employed by Hughes in other works. It is still strong and uncompromising. The collection is peopled with animals and myths, images are often disturbing, and there is a strong sense of turbulence.

In 'Red', the last poem in the collection, Hughes explores the many connotations of red, which was 'your colour'. Here we are presented with a kaleidoscope of blood, bones, Aztec temples, lips, poppies, salvias, veins, arteries and roses. The roses 'drip' and 'weep'. He says she wrapped red around her. Red is the rage and pain she held inside her and it represents her inner psychological 'bleeding'. The red is contrasted with Plath's other colour, white. The white of bones, and clinics. The poem ends with a different colour, blue: the colour of the bluebird which sometimes appeared in Plath's imagery, at least metaphorically. The bluebird of hope, of comfort, of guardian angels. Hughes finishes the poem, and the collection, with the line 'But the jewel that you lost was blue.' One gets the feeling that Hughes is saying that he, too, knows what he has lost.

Birthday Letters is the closest that we get to autobiography in Hughes's work. However, the wary reader will avoid a literal interpretation of every poem, which is, after all, an attempt by Hughes to create his own myth, and will seek other things in the poetry; the themes, ideas and obsessions which drove Hughes, helping him to become the most respected male poet of his generation.

✳ ✳ ✳ *SUMMARY* ✳ ✳ ✳

- *Birthday Letters* is Hughes's answer to his critics.

- It is a personal response and is confessional in tone.

- Its language is as powerful as ever but the tone is rather more reflective.

- It allows Hughes to 'close' a painful chapter in his life by exploring it and coming to terms with it.

8 Reactions to Hughes's Work

> Often the poet has moved forward in a kind of darkness or twilight. The critic covers the same ground with a lamp in his hand and illuminates the path.
>
> (Eugene Ionesco, 'A Writer's Problems', *Encounter*, Sept. 1964)

SEEING CLOSE UP

Ted Hughes died in 1998 and so his work is still very close to us. In some senses it is difficult to know what we think of him because we don't yet have the benefit of hindsight or historical context. When a living writer presents us with a new work, we sometimes struggle to know what we think about it and this has been the case with Hughes throughout his writing life.

In the case of Ted Hughes, we can consult him constantly about his work. He has left an enormous amount of material which states his purposes and gives us the background to his ideas. In articles, radio broadcasts, conference papers and books, he has left many clues as to his intentions.

All this is to the good and can be very helpful, but it can also cloud our judgement and obscure the 'facts'. The writer may not intend to deceive but it is difficult to see ourselves as others see us. Like the rest of us, writers can only report the world from one viewpoint – their own.

That is why we turn to reviewers and critics. As Ionesco points out, the good commentator can shed light on a text that may have blind spots for the person who wrote it. If we accept that individuals all use language slightly differently, and that there is no set of concrete meanings to any word or set of words, we can also accept that writers may occasionally be deluded or blind to what they have written.

Reviewers of Hughes have always been divided in their reaction to his work, but the public, particularly through the English education system, have been introduced to Hughes since they were very young.

THE POPULARITY OF HUGHES

Kate Clanchy, who has obviously taught Hughes on school syllabuses for many years, lists the amazing penetration of Hughes into the teaching of English in English Secondary Schools:

> ... primary pupils will read at least *The Iron Man* and probably *Meet my Folks!* during Literacy Hour ... they may go on to study some poems from the Hughes and Heaney edited *The Rattle Bag* during Years 7 and 8 ... This will be followed with 'Hawk Roosting' in Year 9, complete with a classroom display of fascist-looking eagles, and a selection of animal poems in Years 10 or 11 ... Other poems studied at this time may well be taken from Hughes and Heaney's National Curriculum conforming volume, *The Schoolbag*. At 'A' level, *Lupercal* and *Crow* are popular set texts – *Crow*, in particular, is a frequent progenitor of black tee-shirt wearing and mounds of execrable teenage verse – while essays comparing 'The Thought-Fox' with Heaney's 'Digging' are so frequently set that you can download dozens from the internet. ... Hughes has, in effect, been nationalised.

> (Kate Clanchy in 'The Nationalisation of Ted Hughes', *Thumbscrew* magazine, issue 14 at www.bris.ac.uk/thumbscrew/thum_rev.html#clanchy)

This is quite an achievement for any poet, especially as his popularity arose while he was still alive and illustrates how much of a chord Hughes has struck. Clanchy is of the opinion that this beatifying is not a good thing for Hughes, or for British poetry, because it may give a message to children that poetry can only describe what is outside their own experience, but she also identifies why Hughes became so popular and why people will continue to teach him:

> ... an apparent escape from politics, gender, psychoanalysis and ourselves; a wish to relocate poetry and the sublime back where the Romantics put it, in a natural England, a world of textures, sounds and creatures which few of us have in fact experienced.

EARLY REVIEWS

Hughes's first collection, *The Hawk in the Rain*, was generally well received although it tended to take people by surprise with its newness and freshness. W. S. Merwin in the *New York Times* of 7 October 1957 obviously warmed to the young poet and admired his 'capacity for incaution' in an age when poetry was 'careful and coffee-spooned'. Merwin describes the poems as having 'an ear, a sense of form and development, and a poetic intelligence, all of a high order'. This, and winning the poetry award in New York were an auspicious and encouraging start.

Edwin Muir found the volume 'a most surprising first book' and he goes on to point out that the images are so strong that the symbolic springs out of them, 'whether it was intended to be there or not' ('Kinds of Poetry', *New Statesman*, vol. 54, 28 September 1957, p. 392).

Muir also found an 'admirable violence' in the poems of *The Hawk in the Rain*, and thus showed an early understanding of what Hughes was trying to achieve. Perhaps like A. Alvarez, he welcomed the break from the anodyne poems of the Movement poets in favour of something more elemental.

Not everyone came to like Hughes and his work, but he made his mark early and kept his work at the forefront of poetry in English throughout his life. Keith Sagar, a long-time commentator on the poet's work, said in 1975 that he felt Hughes to be a great poet because:

> he possesses the kind of imagination which issues the purest poetry, charged poetry, visionary, revelatory poetry that sees into the life of things, that takes over where all other modes falter. Words, though controlled up to a point, are allowed to retain a life of their own and express more than the poet consciously knows. His imagination draws on the racial unconscious, on his sixth sense and perhaps innumerable further senses, speaks through him.

> (Sagar, *The Art of Ted Hughes*, Introduction p. 3)

THE LOSS OF THE LYRICAL

As collections were published, the critics and reviewers queued up to have their say. They basically fell into two camps: those who found the poetry too violent, or unstructured, or fatalistic, or just plain flawed; and those who really appreciated what Hughes was trying to achieve.

The favourable reception of both *The Hawk in the Rain* and *Lupercal* began to change as he pushed language harder and harder. Eavan Boland, writing in 1999, felt that *Crow* was a diminution of Hughes's powers.

> Suddenly, with *Crow* in 1970, he seemed to lose his way. The poet of England and accuracy, of the magic fox and the dreaming pike, had disappeared. The volume was turned up; rhetoric replaced clear language; Gothic overstatement did the work of lyricism.
>
> (Eaven Boland, 'Ted Hughes: A Reconciliation', *New York Times*, 24 Jan. 1999, at www.nytimes.com/books/99/01/bookend/bookend.html)

This was one of Hughes's main problems. His first two outstanding early collections had their roots in the English pastoral tradition, albeit with a harsher edge. Some of his audience found themselves unable to shift ground when he decided to push the boundaries of what poetry could do. The sense of the loss of the lyrical among some of Hughes's followers did Hughes some harm, but in the long term he has survived his early expectations and has produced some of England's finest poetry.

RE-EVALUATION

Hughes's reputation is currently undergoing a re-evaluation, forced by the publication of *Birthday Letters* and by his death. John Redmond and Alan Sillitoe, albeit friends of Hughes, in an obituary, saw him as 'a critic of the mainstream Western culture, particularly of the utilitarian rationalism arising from the Enlightenment. In this he is in line with such people as William Blake, W. B. Yeats and D. H. Lawrence.' They go on to point out that his sharp sense of humour has not been sufficiently acknowledged, and that he transformed the post-war scene in Britain (John Redmond and Alan Sillitoe, 'Poets of the Spirits of the Land', *Guardian*, 30 October 1998 at www.guardian.co.uk/departments/ poetry/story/0,6000,102005,00.html).

Eaven Boland, herself an avowed critic of Hughes's apparent attempt to rewrite his relationship with Plath, concedes in the article mentioned above, that it is time to drop some of the old baggage: 'Now that they are not, everything they achieved is unhurt.'

Birthday Letters initially brought out the old polarities. Sarah Lyall reviews some of the contemporary reactions to the book in 'A Divided Response to Poems of Ted Hughes', *New York Times*, 27 January 1998 at www.nytimes.com/library/books/012798hughes-poetry-art.html.

Some people read Hughes in a cynical light.

Some feminists tended to regard the book as a whitewash, or at least a flawed account. In particular, they deride Hughes for seeing Plath's death as inevitable and her instability as being paramount in the relationship. Some people have never forgiven him for leaving out of *Ariel* some of the poems most damning of himself, editing out bits from Plath's journals, destroying the final volume and 'losing' other bits. They see the *Birthday Letters* as being a further denial of his own culpability in her death.

Reaction remains mixed on the merits of the work. Tom Paulin regards it as a great book, 'It's like walking on ice reading it' (quoted in Sarah Lyall). Susan R. van Dyne, a Plath scholar, is quoted in the same article as saying 'These poems are the fiction that Hughes as a survivor has needed to create over the past 35 years.'

Out of the arguments, one thing is clear. Ted Hughes is an artist who provokes strong reactions. It is these reactions that have kept the literary world discussing Hughes the poet, and it is these reactions which will fuel interest in Hughes for many years to come.

✳ ✳ ✳ *SUMMARY* ✳ ✳ ✳

● Hughes's first two collections were hailed by critics as being something new.

● As he experimented further with language and form, opinion became divided.

● The circumstances of Plath's death and Hughes subsequent behaviour made him enemies and clouded judgements about his worth as a poet.

● *Birthday Letters* began a reappraisal of Hughes which is ongoing.

Critical Approaches

9

LANGUAGE AND LINGUISTICS

Structuralism and Post-structuralism

As we have seen, Hughes was very concerned with the language that poets use. And the way Hughes uses language has always fascinated those who have commented upon him. The main thinking about language comes from the work of the structuralists and post-structuralists.

Structuralism

This grew from the ideas of Claude Lévi-Strauss and Roland Barthes who looked at language as a set of structures which only have meaning in relationship to each other. Using the ideas of Ferdinand de Saussure they set out to find laws or structures which governed the text as a whole. This is an approach which places less emphasis on 'meaning' than on relationships within the structures of a text.

Post-structuralism

From these ideas came those of the post-structuralists, who developed the idea that it is language that shapes the world. Given that language can have no set 'correct' meaning, the world becomes an uncertain place. We saw in 'Major Themes' how Hughes struggled to define the crowiness of a crow, and the struggle he had with language to make it happen, and, of course, he discovered that language is inadequate for the tasks it sets out to achieve. Once you have attempted to describe or define something, you have already changed it.

The Symbolic order

We have already seen that Hughes regarded himself as a shaman, someone who understood culture at a very deep level and who could connect the past and the current through an examination of the unconscious cultural system of representations. For example, Western civilization is largely a Christian-based culture which is dominated by

representations of the godhead. These include
the figure of Christ on the cross, blood and
sacrifice, the resurrection, etc. Linked to this
are other myths and representations, forming
what Jacques Lacan calls the **Symbolic order**.

By using ancient myth, and by creating new
myths based upon it, Hughes was trying to
find a way of expressing modern perceptions
as a part of that deep and lasting culture, or
perhaps trying to help heal by allowing a reconnection with that
Symbolic order.

> **KEYWORD**
>
> Symbolic order: The way
> symbols are used
> unconsciously by a
> culture and thus a way of
> 'unlocking' a culture.
> Different societies may
> have different symbolic
> orders and this can lead
> to misunderstanding.

One of the best insights into the way Hughes uses language is *The
Poetry of Ted Hughes, Language, Illusion and Beyond*, by Paul Bentley.
He employs the work of the structuralists and post-structuralists,
particularly Lacan, Kristeva and Barthes to illustrate how Hughes uses
language in his poetry. In his introduction to the book, he postulates
that:

> the poems display a marked uneasiness (and by the same token
> playfulness) with language as a means of representation itself, more
> often than not calling attention to the act of representation itself, in
> other words, the creative act: it is as if the act of creating meaning is the
> significant thing here, over and above the signified meanings of the
> poems.
>
> (Bentley, *The Poetry of Ted Hughes*, Introduction, p. 1)

He goes on to examine Hughes's use of language in a variety of
conceptual ways, showing that the poet was very aware of what he was
doing. By the time we got to *Moortown Diary*, Bentley argues, Hughes
has stopped trying to express the Real in terms of language and myth
alone and has begun 'to wrench some sort of meaning from a world
that resists human projections' (op. cit. p. 103). In other words,
however humans attempt to explain the world, it remains inexplicable.
The most useful way of dealing with life is to do what Hughes does in
'Tractor', and personify the machine:

there is something heroic about the whole procedure: in being humanised, life is being made more manageable, as if it were in this very process of imaginative projection (against the odds) of human meaning (into a void) that our humanity as such resided ... (op. cit. p. 103).

We may take issue with Bentley here and argue that Hughes has merely found another way of expressing living with the Real: after all, you can often describe something by what it isn't, as well as by trying to define what it is. However, the whole book is an illuminating look at what Hughes was trying to achieve and how he set about achieving it.

PASTORAL AND POST-PASTORAL

Ted Hughes is often represented as a 'nature poet', in the tradition of John Clare or D. H. Lawrence. However, it would be simplistic to define him simply in these terms. Undoubtedly he can be placed in the **pastoral** tradition, but in fact, it is more useful to see him as post-pastoral.

Terry Gifford spells out what the main characteristics of post-pastoral literature are. These include the recognition of a universe equally in balance between birth and death, death and rebirth, growth and decay; a recognition that our inner nature can be understood through our relationship to outer nature; and that the corollary of consciousness is conscience. In fact, Gifford sets out six tenets of post-pastoralism which, by definition, are the same as a rising new star in the field of academic literary studies, that of ecocriticism (Gifford, 'Pastoral, Anti-pastoral and Post-pastoral', in L. Coupe (ed.), *The Green Studies Reader, From Romanticism to Ecocriticism*, Routledge, 2000, p. 221).

> **KEYWORD**
>
> Pastoral: In literary terms, a mode of writing which concerns itself with nature. It is usually nostalgic in tone and harks back to happier days. Pastoral poets include Wordsworth and the Romantics, A. E. Housman and John Clare.

ECOCRITICISM

In the last three decades of the twentieth century, growing in parallel with the environmental movement, came the development of ecocriticism or green studies.

It grew up as a reaction to the heady theorizing of academics, particularly those who buried themselves deep in the world of language and semiotics, calling themselves structuralists, post-structuralists and post-modernists, and arguing that there was no meaning to be found in texts, or that the author was dead. Some 1990s' ecocritics jokingly called themselves 'compost-structuralists' to distance themselves from the intellectual posturings of those critics and to emphasize a connection with more earthy matters.

Ecocriticism aims to reconnect humankind with the power which sustains it. It counters any notion that nature is a construct or function of language. Ecocritics might argue for example that the daffodils in Wordsworth's famous poem are not just the constructs of a poet, serving to stand as symbols for beauty, the life/death cycle or the poetic vision: they are first and foremost plants which exist without language and they are part of something greater than humankind.

Robert Pogue Harrison outlines a view of the role of the poet in ecocritical terms:

> As the external environment undergoes transformations, poets often announce them in advance with the clairvoyance of seers, for poets have an altogether sixth sense that enables them to forecast trends in the weather, so to speak. Like oracles, they couch their message in the language of enigma. And like oracles, the meaning of their message becomes fully manifest only after the events it foretells have unfolded. Modern poetry at its best is a kind of spiritual ecology.

(Robert Pogue Harrison, 'The Forest of Literature', in Coupe, p.217)

Following the analogy of the earth becoming an ecological and spiritual wasteland, he argues that T. S. Eliot foreshadowed much of what was to come in *The Waste Land*, and traces the representation of the new poverty of spirit and language up to Samuel Beckett whose 'bleak, minimalist' language reflects the current state of human affairs – an existence in an exploited world where 'real' or 'natural' values have become subservient to human arrogance. Ecocriticism engages with the consequences of the technological age, exposing the intellectual arrogance which characterizes it.

An ecocritical reading of Ted Hughes would therefore see him in terms of being a spiritual ecologist, and perhaps an oracle, acting as a mirror to a society blind to its own doings. This ties in directly with Hughes's own notion of the role (his role) of the shaman. He used words like 'Technosphere' to describe a kind of anti-nature, a propensity in man which seems intent on violating, controlling and heedlessly destroying the very fabric which keeps him alive.

We have seen how in *Crow*, Hughes examines the whole of Western civilization by setting up a bleak, barren landscape where the dramas unfold. Hughes, like Hardy, uses landscape to indicate metaphorical and **allegorical** worlds but unlike Hardy, rejects comparison with the

> **KEYWORD**
>
> Post-modernism: In the mid-late twentieth century a reaction set in to the artistic and cultural movement called modernism. (In architecture, people like Le Corbusier stood for modernism, and in literature, such people as T. S. Eliot and D. H. Lawrence.) The distinguishing features of post-modernism are an eclectic approach – taking influences from all periods and cultures; parody and pastiche. But in some ways, the term merely means 'living after modernism' and as such reflects a desire to find new means of expression and new ways of interacting with the world.

beautiful (or the nostalgic pastoral past) and concentrates on the ugliness of the world created through human notions of progress. We see the theme spelled out clearly in a poem from *Cave Birds* 'She Seemed So Considerate':

> … the bird came
> She said: 'Your world has died.'
> It sounded so dramatic. (p. 70 TB)

The irony of 'It sounded so dramatic' satirizes the prevailing attitude of the developed world where changes to nature hardly seem relevant or important. The persona in the poem goes on to say that his potted fern has died, 'the one fellow spirit I still cherished'.

Terry Gifford, in *The Green Studies Reader*, also takes his example from *Cave Birds*. The cockerel protagonist is placed on trial for neglect of his inner self, which has meant 'his alienation from the forces of nature in himself and outside himself'. The cockerel is an apt symbol of humanity given his overbearing arrogance. Gifford quotes Hughes himself in a 1975 radio broadcast saying: 'His own self, finally, the innate nature of his flesh and blood, brings him to court' (op. cit. p. 221).

Much of Hughes's work can be seen as taking a stand against **anthropocentrism**, against the notion that all is measured through the eyes of man. His later poems, such as those in *Moortown Diary*, do not take the stance of the superior or ironic observer, but rather show man back in the landscape, interacting with nature and nurturing his animals, rather than interfering and destroying.

> ## KEYWORDS
>
> **Allegory:** A story in which a meaning beyond the obvious one is represented symbolically. John Bunyan's *Pilgrim's Progress* is an allegory of man's quest for salvation told as an adventure story. George Orwell's *Animal Farm* is told as a simple fable about animals trying to take control of their lives and destinies. Yet it is also, on one level, an allegory of Soviet Communism, and on another, of how power and greed have corrupted mankind.
>
> **Anthropocentrism:** The perceiving of the natural world (or a deity) as having human characteristics and feelings to the point where only the human perspective matters.

ECOFEMINISM

An integral and interesting recent development is the fusion of feminist studies with ecocriticism.

The use of feminine pronouns to describe nature goes back a long way, and we are very used to talking about 'Mother Nature'. The feminine qualities ascribed include motherhood (creation), nurturing (tending creation) and homemaking (keeping order through domestic tasks). Nature is often seen to be vulnerable, adaptable and, above all, biddable. And it is biddable by the will of men.

Throughout the late 1960s and the first half of the 1970s, the hippy movement created and spread the icon of the earth mother, and thus enslaved many women in this trap while promising a new liberation through a reconnection with the soil. At one level, ecofeminism seeks to explore this while keeping its most convenient features. It also works from the notion that the exploitation of the planet is of the same nature as the exploitation of women and minorities.

Feminine and masculine in Hughes's work

Feminism has long had a grudge against Hughes. After Plath's death he was seen by many feminists as an absolute monster, a brute who killed their heroine through cruelty and betrayal. Feelings were so strong that the surname Hughes was erased from her gravestone. His poetry too seems to emphasize the masculine. The images in his poetry are violent, often brutal and disturbing. The world of *Crow*, for example, has little of the feminine – it is men (including a strongly male God) who battle for the world and pick over the pieces. It is men who wage wars in Hughes's war poetry, and the natural world is represented by strong, dangerous beasts who cannot be tamed. We generally assume in Hughes's poetry, unless he indicates to the contrary, that the jaguar, owl, hawk or fox in question is male (or at least demonstrates male traits).

Indeed, the Crow myth invented by Hughes has, as its denouement, an old hag testing Crow until he gets his answers right, whereupon she turns into a beautiful young woman and they run off happily into the woods. A typical male fantasy if ever there was one – and yet Hughes wasn't merely indulging in male wish-fulfilment: he equates such figures with the matriarchal principle of *The White Goddess*, as we have already seen.

Energy and power

In 1987 Dennis Walder tried to anticipate feminist arguments over the apparent phallocentricity of Hughes's vision by mounting the defence that Hughes's work was not that of male dominated violence and egocentricity, but was 'better understood as an emphasis on energy and power'. This is in tune with Hughes's own thinking.

Walder argues that in order to understand the patriarchal view of society at that time, Hughes needed to express maleness. He goes on to explore the rise of the feminine in Hughes's later work by comparing the masculine world of *Crow* with some of the *Moortown Diary* poems, in particular 'Prospero and Sycorax' (pp. 206-7). The 'she' referred to is Sycorax, witch, and mother to Caliban from Shakespeare's *The Tempest*, whose powers are brought under control by Prospero.

> Here, the 'Shakespearian fable' identifies the banishment of the life-giving, the sensual, female urge, whose 'knowledge' resides in an awareness of all that is lost of her power by enslavement to the male.
>
> (Dennis Walder, op. cit. p. 81)

In this poem everybody loses, because she knows

> He has found
> something
> easier to live with –
>
> His death, and her death.

Of course there is more than one answer to any question in the debate. In a poetry reading at the Adelaide Festival in March 1986, Hughes acknowledges that the hag's questions in the Crow myth are all about 'the relationship between man and woman – or Man and Woman. So they're all really love questions. And they're all dilemma questions, because they don't have an answer.' ('Ted Hughes at the Adelaide Festival Writer's Week, March 1986', transcribed by Ann Skea at www.zeta.org.au/~annskea/Adelaide.htm.)

Exploitation of the feminine

Ecofeminists like Louise H. Westling worry about the way gender and landscape have become interlinked in ecofeminism so that the longstanding tradition of ascribing the feminine to nature and the masculine to its exploiters is reinforced: 'That's absurd,' she is reported as saying, 'The land is not a woman. But from ancient times, writers have used feminine images to justify conquering it' (in 'Scholars Embark on a Study of Literature About the Environment', *The Chronicle of Higher Education*, 9 August 1996, at www.asle.umn.edu/archive/intro/chronicle.html).

Against dualism

Karla Ambruster argues the complexity of the whole issue and makes a plea against the use of simple dualisms and the use of hierarchies (man bad/nature good) in favour of an approach 'that complicates cultural conceptions of human identity and human relationships with non-human nature rather than relying on unproblematized visions of continuity or difference...' ('A Poststructuralist Approach to Ecofeminist Criticism', in L. Coupe (ed.) *The Green Studies Reader*, (pp. 198-9).

It is obvious that simplistic dualist approaches to Hughes can bring about both sympathetic and unsympathetic reactions. Hughes's reliance on the white goddess as a model of the universe is likely to upset some ecofeminists who would see this as a throwback to patriarchal times. The emphasis on the feminine qualities of gentleness, caring and passivity would be seen as a form of oppression by maleness.

On the other hand, other ecofeminists, starting from the principle that it is the feminine that mediates and works for peace and a non-exploitative culture, will argue that Hughes is correct in saying that the world lost its way when the feminine was subjugated to the masculine. The Greenham protestors of the 1980s were certainly acting on the premise that feminine values can oppose and eventually triumph over the masculine.

Towards integration

Hughes is not consciously working in a dualistic way; his vision is of oneness. It is the vision in his Crow myth, in which the two sides of humanity need to find each other and find harmony through union. Adam needs his Eve and Eve needs her Adam. Man is redeemed in Hughes's world by harsh struggle and an eventual union of the yin with the yang. At the same time, Hughes's vision is in step with that of the ecofeminists such as Ambruster, because he too would argue against dualism, and he too would be seeking a new way of relating to nature which was integrated, thoughtful, and meaningful.

* * *SUMMARY* * *

Currently, the main critical attention on Ted Hughes is focused on:

- His use of language as a tool for expressing the inexpressible

- Ecological and ethical concerns

- Feminist issues.

Where to Next?

10

READ SOME HUGHES

The first task of any Hughes student is to read his work. The chronology of major works which follows this chapter will give some clues. Once you have begun to get interested you will find your own way through his works, picking out what interests you or corresponds to themes in which you are interested.

Hughes's major work of non-fiction is *Shakespeare and the Goddess of Complete Being* (Faber & Faber, 1992), in which he re-evaluates Shakespeare in terms of myth. It provides a useful insight into Hughes's thinking as well as being fascinating about Shakespeare's imaginative world.

If you would like to read some of his children's literature, try *The Iron Man* and *The Iron Woman,* before dipping into his many other stories and poems. In 1995 Faber republished a delightful set of four books called *Ted Hughes Collected Animal Poems: Volumes 1–4.* The first volume consists of his poems for very young children and the other volumes are arranged to take a reader into more adult themes. Volume 4 contains many of Hughes's famous adult animal poems.

Occasionally some of Hughes's plays are performed and it is worth getting to see them if you can.

GET TO KNOW SYLVIA PLATH

If you are interested in the Hughes–Plath relationship, you will find Plath's poetry, especially in *Ariel,* casts a strong light on what was going on in her mind and between husband and wife. Perhaps the most famous poem is 'Daddy' which can be read in conjunction with others in *Ariel* and Hughes's *Birthday Letters.* Erica Wagner has produced a very useful companion to *Birthday Letters* entitled *Ariel's Gift – Ted Hughes, Sylvia Plath and the Story of Birthday Letters.*

A study of Plath will give insight into Hughes, and Tracy Brain's *The Other Sylvia Plath* makes an excellent read.

PLACES TO VISIT

Those wishing to get more of a feel for Hughes could visit Hughes's Yorkshire and Devon. Lumb Bank (Hebden Bridge) is available to students of writing as part of the Arvon Foundation's creative writing programme. Mytholmroyd is worth visiting to see the 'cliff' which so influenced Hughes from his early childhood.

ORGANIZATIONS

Earth | Moon is an interesting Ted Hughes site full of reviews, articles, lists and other information. It is the first port of call for those interested in learning more about Hughes and his work. It can be found at www.uni-leipzig.de/~angl/hughes/index2.htm

Similarly, Ann Skea runs a good site at www.zeta.org.au/~annskea/Default.html

GLOSSARY

Allegory A story in which a meaning beyond the obvious one is represented symbolically. John Bunyan's *Pilgrim's Progress* is an allegory of man's quest for salvation told as an adventure story. George Orwell's *Animal Farm* is told as a simple fable about animals trying to take control of their lives and destinies. Yet it is also, on one level, an allegory of Soviet Communism, and on another, of how power and greed have corrupted mankind.

Anthropocentrism The perceiving of the natural world (or a deity) as having human characteristics and feelings to the point where only the human perspective matters.

Archetype Literally a prototype from our ancient collective unconscious. Certain qualities such as bravery become embodied in character types which we all recognize. Hero figures are often archetypal in their birth, life story and characteristics. The clichéd use of archetype, without freshness or originality, becomes a stereotype.

Cabbalah A system of symbol and number based on the Jewish mystical scheme of theology and metaphysics.

Confessional writing Poetry or prose where the subject is subjective and personal. The work of Robert Lowell and some of his American contemporaries became known as 'confessional poetry'.

Film noire A stylistic device in film or television which uses dark, brooding, atmospheric lighting effects to increase a sense of danger, or the pervasion of evil forces. Recent examples include Ridley Scott's *Bladerunner* and many scenes in *The X-Files*.

Georgian poetry A term now used pejoratively to refer to the worst of poetry written in the early part of the twentieth century. Such poetry is much criticized for its pastoral and escapist style.

Half- rhyme Basically a rhyme which does not match perfectly but contains enough syllables or consonants to create a similar sound pattern. Largely a twentieth-century device to avoid the irritation sometimes caused by exactly 'chiming' rhymes.

Individuation A Jungian concept which describes the process of integrating the various parts of the personality to become a whole person.

Irony Where the reader perceives a discrepancy between words and meaning. Typically we say one thing when we mean another. A version of this occurs when a character does or says something which they interpret in one way, while the reader, knowing more than the character, can see things entirely differently. Usually, but not always, it is clear that the character is deluded.

Lack A feeling of missing something we greatly value. In the child it is the absence of the mother figure, and in adults it is anything which we feel makes us less than whole.

Metaphor A poetic device whereby an object or image comes to represent something it is not but with which it shares seemingly common characteristics.

Modernism In literature, a broad movement of writers including T. S. Eliot, Pound, Joyce, Woolf, Yeats and D. H. Lawrence. It was informed by the works of Freud and was characterized by a persistent experimentation with language and form. Stream of consciousness is one of its major techniques as well as dependence upon poetic image and myth.

Movement A post-war movement of British poets whose poetry is sardonic, lucid and self-consciously ironic, '… meticulously crafted and witty, controlled and common-sensical' (*Bloomsbury Guide to English Literature*, 1989). The major poets include Thom Gunn, Elizabeth Jennings, Philip Larkin and John Wain.

Nihilism A denial of traditional values, including moral and social ones, which threatens to topple a prevailing order.

Pastoral In literary terms, a mode of writing which concerns itself with nature. It is usually nostalgic in tone and harks back to happier days. Pastoral poets include Wordsworth and the Romantics, A. E. Housman and John Clare.

Personification Where animals, objects, places or ideas are given human characteristics – turned into a character which thinks in human ways.

Post-modernism In the mid-late twentieth century a reaction set in to the artistic and cultural movement called modernism. The distinguishing features of post-modernism are an eclectic approach – taking influences from all periods and cultures; parody and pastiche. But in some ways, the term merely means 'living after modernism' and as such reflects a desire to find new means of expression and new ways of interacting with the world.

Romantic movement A movement in Britain and Europe roughly between 1770 and 1848. In literary terms it expressed the self and the value of individual experience along with a strong sense of the transcendental. The movement is characterized by such writers as Rousseau, Wordsworth, Mary Wollstonecraft, Coleridge, Byron and Shelley. The motif of the movement was 'Imagination' and it had a belief in the close links between man and nature.

Shaman In tribal cultures, someone who has tested himself to the utmost limits, has shed everything about himself, and has come back as a visionary and healer, exploring the spiritual unconsciousness of the tribe he serves.

Symbolic order The way symbols are used unconsciously by a culture and thus a way of 'unlocking' a culture. Different societies may have different symbolic orders and this can lead to misunderstanding.

Talmud The collection of Jewish religious and civil law. It contains moral doctrine and ritual based on the Scriptures. Second only to the Bible in Jewish religious life.

Chronology of major works

1992   *Shakespeare and the Goddess of Complete Being*
       Rain-Charm for the Duchy and Other Laureate Poems
       A Dancer to God. Tributes to T. S. Eliot
1993   *The Mermaid's Purse. Collected Animal Poems* (for children)
       Three Books: Remains of Elmet, Cave Birds, River
       The Iron Woman (for children)
1994   *Elmet*
       Winter Pollen. Occasional Prose
1995   *New Selected Poems: 1957–1994*
       The Dreamfighter and Other Creation Tales (for children)
       Difficulties of a Bridegroom. Collected Short Stories
       Collected Animal Poems
       Frank Wedekind: Spring Awakening in a New Version by Ted Hughes
1996   *Federico García Lorca: Blood Wedding. In a New Version by Ted Hughes*
       Tales from Ovid
       Shaggy and Spotty (for children)
1998   *Birthday Letters*
       Jean Racine: Phèdre. A New Version by Ted Hughes
1999   *The Oresteia of Aeschylus: A New Translation by Ted Hughes*
       Euripides: Alcestis. In a Version by Ted Hughes

BIBLIOGRAPHY AND FURTHER READING

General introductions

Keith Sagar, *The Art of Ted Hughes*, Faber, 1980

Dennis Walder, *Ted Hughes*, Open University Press, 1987

Gina Wisker, *Sylvia Plath A Beginner's Guide*, Hodder & Stoughton, 2001

Academic texts

Paul Bentley, *The Poetry of Ted Hughes, Language, Illusion and Beyond*, Longman, 1998

Tracy Brain, *The Other Sylvia Plath*, Pearson, 2001

Terry Gifford and Neil Roberts, *Ted Hughes A Critical Study*, Faber & Faber 1981

Keith Sagar, *The Laughter of Foxes*, Liverpool University Press, 2000

Ecocriticism

Laurence Coupe (ed.), *The Green Studies Reader – From Romanticism to Ecocriticism*, Routledge, 2000

Biography

Elaine Einstein, *Ted Hughes The Life of a Poet*, Weidenfeld & Nicolson, 2001

Lucas Myers, *Crow Steered, Bergs Appeared. A Memoir of Ted Hughes and Sylvia Plath*, Proctor's Hall Press, 2001

Anne Stevenson, *Bitter Fame – A Life of Sylvia Plath*, Penguin, 1989.

INDEX